DATE DUE

W9-CBN-577

Stability amid Change

Georgia Harkness

STABILITY AMID CHANGE

ABINGDON PRESS
Nashville and New York

STABILITY AMID CHANGE

Copyright © 1969 by Abingdon Press

Library of Congress Catalog Card Number: 69-12019

Scripture quotations unless otherwise noted are
from the Revised Standard Version of the Bible,
copyrighted 1946 and 1952 by the Division of
Christian Education, National Council of Churches,
and are used by permission.

Portions of Chapter 6, "The New Morality,"
originally appeared in "How New Is the New
Morality?" copyright 1967 by The Christian Century Foundation. Reprinted by permission from the
November, 1967, issue of *The Pulpit*.

Chapter 8, "Toward a Theology of Social
Change," originally appeared in the Winter, 1967,
issue of *Religion in Life*. Copyright 1967 by Abingdon Press.

SET UP, PRINTED, AND BOUND BY THE
PARTHENON PRESS, AT NASHVILLE,
TENNESSEE, UNITED STATES OF AMERICA

To

The Oncoming Generation

"... *your young men shall see visions,*
and your old men shall dream dreams."

Foreword

If there is one thing that is obvious today, it is that in almost every aspect of human life we are living in a time of "the shaking of the foundations." A few years ago the World Council of Churches conducted a significant study of areas of rapid social change, these areas being viewed primarily as the newly emerging nations. Now it is apparent that rapid social change is going on virtually everywhere and that not the least among these spheres of transition is the United States of America.

These changes so affect our political, economic, intellectual, and community life that nobody lives without being to some degree touched by them. The effects are evident; the causes are complex and often intricately interwoven. It would require a very large book—indeed, many books—to give more than a superficial analysis of the current social situation. This is not the aim of this book. Its purpose, rather, is to make some assessment of the accompanying changes in the religious scene and in particular to look at modes of understanding, appropriating, and proclaiming the perennial insights of the Christian gospel within these changing times.

It is clear that we cannot live in the past. Yet we must not reject the past as if it had never been.

Those of us who are Christians have much cause to be grateful for the great tradition of our faith in which the church has long been nourished and of which we are the heirs. Whatever may be thought today of the proper balance between Scripture and tradition, between doctrine and deeds of service, between institutional forms and Christian experience, we need them all. And without these in conjunction through many centuries it is doubtful that either the church or the Christian religion would exist today.

However, it is hardly a wise or helpful procedure to cling to the forms and verbiage of the past as if we did not know that a new day is here. The Christian gospel is timeless; it must ever be adapted to new times. Nostalgia for a past that will not return is never the best mood in which to serve the present age. Nor is anything gained by deploring the only too obvious evils of our time without due recognition of much that is right with modern life. There are signs of new life among the young, in the churches, in race relations, in education and government, among the oppressed, and in emerging nations. We do well to rejoice in these and in the marvelous scientific achievements which, as they open doors to better ways of living among the earth's many millions, serve potentially the goals of Christian love for all God's sons.

In short, we should welcome the new day gladly, not in rebellion or in self-pity, because churches, like other institutions, are being challenged to change with the movements of the times. Yet, it is hardly a good thing to be so contemporary that we forget our debt to the faith that carried our fathers through many a dark day, times that seemed to them every bit as tragic and uncertain as ours, and often more so. This faith bore them forward in fidelity to the call of God and with hope for the future, and it can again give us buoyancy and steadfastness in our time.

This has long been my conviction as I have watched the currents of change over a considerable span of years. But that I should attempt to write a book on the theme of stability amid change came about from a particular circumstance. In rather close conjunction I was asked to participate in two series of lectures: the Annual Fall Lectureship of the Central Christian Church of San Antonio, Texas, in October, 1967, and the Barton Lectures at the Boston Avenue Methodist Church in Tulsa, Oklahoma, in January, 1968. Each occasion called for six presentations. Accordingly, the first six chapters of this book were written in preparation for the San Antonio addresses, revised somewhat, and given again at Tulsa. To the Rev. Myron W. Chrisman, pastor of the Central Christian Church, to Mrs. L. S. Barton, donor of the second lectureship, and to Dr. Finis A. Crutchfield, her pastor in the Boston Avenue Methodist Church, I am deeply indebted—not only for these invitations, but for many acts of courtesy and the warm fellowship of their people on these occasions.

As the reader will observe, the lectures dealt with the nature of the Christian gospel, the state of the church and guidelines for its renewal, the Bible and its place in the modern world, prayer and its possibilities and problems today, the newer currents of theology, and the new morality. A seventh chapter seemed to be called for to deal more inclusively with the relation of the churches to the world in view of the attention presently being given to secularity. Then to round off the book the publishers and I decided to add "Toward a Theology of Social Change," which had been published in the Winter, 1967, issue of *Religion in Life*.

I am dedicating this book to the oncoming generation, for it is they who must carry forward the abiding elements of the Christian gospel amid the conditions of the unborn future. Disturbed though they often are by the nature of the world they have inherited, I do not despair of them. Their zeal for a better world is high, and there is ground to stand on if they will find it. Such stability is finally grounded not in changing social structures, though these are of no slight importance, but in the vision of the young man of Galilee who died, still young, outside a city wall.

Contents

Contents

1

The Good News of God

The world is full of bad news. As we read the newspaper or listen to the news by radio or television, who is there who has not occasionally remarked, "I wish they would tell us good news once in awhile!" To be sure, the vocation of newscasters is to tell us the unusual, and the fact that so much is unmentioned as life moves on in a relatively even tenor in many thousands of homes and communities is a silent tribute to the fact that not all is wrong in our world. Nevertheless, there is plenty of bad news. The war in Vietnam as it drags on its tragic, death-dealing way; the unsolved problems of the Middle East and many tensions elsewhere; a rising crime rate; a steadily increasing divorce rate and slipping sexual standards; increasing addiction to alcohol and drugs; death on the highways and in the air and from riots that destroy both life and property; murder and suicide at every level of society—these are among the things that fill the news.

Add to these matters in which human agency is present the hurricanes, floods, and earthquakes which the insurance policies ironically call "acts of God," and the problem of unexplained evil is upon us in full force. Add, further, to these outward, newsworthy occurrences the inner anxieties, the frustration, the insecurity, the loneliness, and

the general "unsettledness" of hosts of people, and
one has a fairly accurate picture of the temper of
the times.

Such news may take new forms, but it is by no
means new. The literature of the ages echoes with
the theme of human suffering, and insofar as this
note has a religious background it often takes the
form of "How long? O Lord, how long?" Not only
is this the main theme of the book of Job, but it
is found in many other passages in the Bible. The
author of the fourth psalm puts it in a capsule
when he writes:

There are many who say, "O that we might see some
    good!
    Lift up the light of thy countenance upon us, O
    Lord!"

It is not my purpose to try to give a neatly
packaged answer to the age-old problem of pain.
I believe it is not wholly unanswerable, for the
greater part of human suffering is the result of
human sin, carelessness, and indifference to the
rights, the needs, and the feelings of others. Some
of it, not humanly caused, can be seen as the result
of the operation of natural forces, such as gravita-
tion and atmospheric pressure, on which our very
existence depends. In keeping with the ancient
biblical injunction to "fill the earth and subdue
it" and to "have dominion" over the things of

nature, it is man's calling to turn both social and natural forces to human good in a world in which creativity continues. Our main concern, however, is not to try to explain why the world is as it is, but to examine the good news of God for living in it.

The gospel means *good news,* or *glad tidings.* One does not ordinarily go to the dictionary for theological definitions, but my dictionary throws light on what the word means. Its first definition of the word *gospel* is "good news or tidings, especially the announcement of the salvation of men through the atoning death of Jesus Christ." I accept this definition, though I should want to include the vivifying life as well as the atoning death of Jesus Christ. Next comes *Gospel* as "the four memoirs of Jesus Christ as contained in the New Testament," a familiar enough meaning as we speak of Matthew, Mark, Luke, and John as the four Gospels. But the word *gospel* has other meanings. I find it defined as "any doctrine concerning human welfare that is agitated as of great importance; as the antislavery gospel"; again "that which is regarded as infallibly true"; and finally "any doctrine in politics, or otherwise, which is strenuously advocated by its supporters." What these definitions say to me is that if, as Christians, we took our gospel as seriously as do the defenders of causes and politicians in their enterprises, both personal and social evils could be radically changed through the good news of Jesus Christ.

There are certain ancient enemies of the human spirit that are as old as the human race. There is pain, both physical and mental, from a great number of causes but never pleasant to endure. There is death, inevitable for all of us and made doubly poignant by the grief which comes from separation from our loved ones. There is what the author of the Letter to the Hebrews called "the sin which clings so closely," or in the older, more vivid translation, "the sin which doth so easily beset us." Sin takes many forms, mounting in the social seriousness of its effects as society becomes more complex and interrelated.

The continuing presence of these ancient factors has given rise to new terminology in the existentialist philosophy and theology of our time. We hear little about sin, but much about alienation and estrangement. One of the most vivid terms to denote this predicament has been brought into relatively common diction from the German by the late Paul Tillich.[1] This is *Angst. Angst* is no surface anxiety or recognizable fear which can be corrected by simply removing its cause; it is a deep inner unrest. It is a state of being ill at ease and seeking without finding at the very depths of one's being. It infects the total person and keeps him

[1] The Danish equivalent was used earlier by Søren Kierkegaard.

from his fullest living. Yet the situation is not without hope. One can be grasped by a good beyond one's self, and while knowing that one is unacceptable, he can feel that he is accepted by the Source of this good.

So far, we seem to be moving in the sphere of depth psychology with which Professor Tillich had a very rich acquaintance. Yet his term for this life-transforming power is the New Being in Jesus as the Christ, which as the object of ultimate concern brings about a new being in the individual. Then accepting responsibility for others, the accepted and changed person is impelled to contribute to the changing of a disordered culture.

This is a profound conception which has had great influence and, on the whole, a constructive influence on many persons in our time who recognize in themselves the *Angst* but do not find it spoken to in the conventional terminology of the churches. However, I do not believe that either the terminology of the Bible or of the mainstream of Christian theology, which calls this experience salvation or redemption, is outdated in our time.

It is significant that a term which for a long time went largely out of fashion in Christian circles seems to be coming back. This is conversion. The July, 1967, issue of *The Ecumenical Review,* a quarterly journal of the World Council of Churches, is devoted almost entirely to eight articles on conversion which came from various parts of the world, and its main theme in the April, 1968, issue is evangelism. The leading theme of another scholarly journal, *Religion in Life,* Summer, 1967, is salvation. Basic to both conversion and salvation is the turning from a self-centered to a God-centered life and the finding of a new power and direction for living, or to use a contemporary phrase, a new "style of living."

Such a process is too wide and deep in its implications to be described properly in a few words. Yet its outlines may be stated. In this reorientation of life, whether sudden or gradual, fear is transcended in faith, despair in hope, self-centeredness in outgoing love. Life receives a new unity, a new wholeness, a new spiritual health. Sin does not disappear, but in penitence and knowledge of forgiveness temptations become easier to master. Pain may remain, but it no longer overwhelms us. Death is still inevitable, but it need no longer be dreaded, and grief finds comfort in the assurance of eternal life. Insofar as conversion or the experience of salvation is deep-going, it changes attitudes in the whole of life, public as well as private, social as well as individual, and the otherwise secular matters of politics, economics, and daily living take on a new sacredness of meaning and sense of Christian obligation.

It is often said today that there is no difference to be discerned between Christians in the churches and secularists outside of them. To some degree this is doubtless true, both because there are good people outside of churches and there are people in churches who are Christians in name only—or not much more than in name. Yet we know persons whose faith and life are a living witness to the gospel. Often humble persons and certainly not perfect ones, they have a way of meeting both the joyous and the painful events of life which marks them unmistakably as Christians.

Paul said it for us when he wrote, "Therefore, if any one is in Christ, he is a new creation; the old has passed away, behold, the new has come." But what does it mean to be "in Christ"? And what was there in Jesus that made his coming in the first century and his presence as the living Christ today such good news that we call it the gospel? These questions have many facets, but I wish to try to answer them together in terms of light in darkness, an almost lost sense of wonder, and love in the midst of a hate-filled, strife-torn world.[2]

In the Old Testament at its highest points of prophetic insight there is a foregleam of a coming Redeemer of whom Isaiah could say, "The people who walked in darkness have seen a great light; and they that dwell in the land of the shadow of death, upon them hath the light shined" (9:2 KJV). Then in due time came the Light of the

[2] In the remainder of this chapter I have used some material, though with revisions, from a sermon of mine entitled, "The Meaning of Advent," which appeared in *The Pulpit Digest* of November, 1953.

world, to be born among the lowly and live among men to bring light to darkened spirits, healing to sick bodies, forgiveness to sick souls, courage to the fearful, strength to the weak, new life to the dull and downcast. When his earthly work was over and it again seemed that gross darkness covered the earth, he rose triumphant over sin and death in the light of the Resurrection morning, and in awareness of his living presence the church was born. A few decades later, when the fires of persecution cast an ominous shadow over the efforts of the early Christians to be faithful and the temptation to inner darkness assailed their spirits, the author of the Fourth Gospel wrote, "In him was life, and the life was the light of men. The light shines in the darkness, and the darkness has not overcome it."

Because the bad news of today has led some to believe that the light of Christian faith is extinguished, let us rapidly review the centuries. The light was still shining in the darkness in the second century, when Christians were being arrested, imprisoned, and put to death for refusing to render to Caesar what belonged to God. It was still shining in the fifth century, when the collapse of the greatest empire on earth put an end to the much trusted political security of the *Pax Romana* and ushered in what history has called the Dark Ages. Dark they were, but not wholly dark, for the light was still shining as the medieval church through its monasteries and parish priests kept the lamp of learning lighted, ministered to the sick and the poor, provided hostels for travelers, and gave much stability to a troubled age. It was still shining in the eleventh and twelfth centuries in spite of the excesses and tragic folly of the Crusades.

The light was still shining in the thirteenth century as the old stabilities of the feudal system began to break up, and it shone on in later centuries amid the horrors of the Inquisition, the strife and bloodshed over religious differences, the splitting up of Protestantism into great numbers of denominations, the emergence of modern science, the birth of capitalism and of nationalism, the scramble of nations for overseas empires, the coming of modern political democracy, the emergence of totalitarian faiths and systems, the deepening of economic and racial tensions, and the changes—for good or ill— that have come with great forward strides in technology and the nuclear/space age.

The light from Christ has continued to shine through persecution, war, and all manner of conflict, and it shines today. Indeed, it shines with a greater glow because of amazing developments in ecumenical fellowship, both within Protestantism and Eastern Orthodoxy and between these groups and Roman Catholicism. It shines in the current emphasis on the laity as the church within the world, called to a ministry of service in every sphere in which their lives are set. It shines in the kind of democracy which stems from the teaching of Jesus about the love of neighbor and the worth of every person in the eyes of God, whatever his race or color, his age or sex or social status. Jesus did not say much about "the dignity of man" or "human brotherhood"—phrases that we bandy about too lightly—but he did something more lasting. What he did was to live by these conceptions; put them into prayers to "our Father" and into matchless parables; mingle with folk of all races and nations and stations in life; minister in God's name to human need wherever need was found. If his light still shines within us, we will do the same.

Another basic note in the good news of God is the wonder that Jesus elicits in responsive souls. We are inclined to marvel at the wonders of science, and well we may, and we may even speak of the miracles it has wrought in our time. But are we not inclined to take Jesus for granted because we have heard about him all our lives? We had better recover something of a lost sense of wonder in our faith.

I do not mean that we should simply marvel at the miracles of Jesus, though we do well to remember that the meaning of a miracle does not hinge on whether it does or does not involve a suspension of natural law. Miracles, by the derivation of the word, are occurrences which fill one with wonder and amazement, and in a religious context they are "God's wonderful works."

Jesus himself is the greatest of all miracles. The stories of the birth of Jesus are great poetry and drama; this is why the beauty of the Christmas pageantry gets hold of the dullest of us. Beyond that, they are great religion, for they proclaim the most wonderful event that ever occurred on this planet. For Jesus to have been born, and to have lived among men as he lived, and to have taught as he taught, and to have died as he died, and to have risen again to dwell with us as Eternal Presence, is a fact before which we too should be filled with wonder and amazement.

It is the major miracle of all time that one whose public ministry lasted three years at the most, who wrote no book and held no office in synagogue or state, who had only a modest formal education, and whose recorded words can all be read easily in an hour, should have become the most influential figure in all history. Indeed, it is remarkable that he escaped oblivion! What chance had he, by any normal expectation, of being heard of outside Nazareth and Jerusalem and parts between? He was a Jew, living in an occupied outpost of the Roman Empire with no means of communication with the center of things; an obscure Jew, of the class of small artisans, whom most people of his day never heard of; who was regarded by most of his contemporaries who knew anything about him either as a wonder-worker or a religious fanatic; who was repudiated by the leaders of his own people and deserted at the last by most of his followers; who was then executed like any common criminal.

What chance had this man of leaving anything behind him? Yet one cannot tell the story of the past nineteen centuries in the Western world and leave Jesus out. One cannot think of great music or great art or great literature and leave Jesus out. His words have impregnated our language and, if we are not too dull, have sensitized our consciences. When we think of all that has come from him in the impulse to human freedom and dignity —the challenging of ignorance; the conquest of disease; the growth of concern for the weak, the destitute, and the helpless; the stabilizing of the inner lives of millions of his followers around the world and the fostering of a prophetic attack on such giant social evils as race prejudice, human injustice, and war—when we simply enumerate such things that have stemmed from his influence, we are dull indeed if the wonder of it does not sweep over our souls.

Yet light and wonder are not the last words. It is when the light from God and the wonder of God's gift in Jesus Christ speak to us reassuringly, then commandingly, of the love of God that by God's grace we become that new creation of which Paul wrote. It is by this that we are led to renewed dedication and thus to new faith and hope and love. In the New Testament we are told that those who heard Jesus speak cried out, "No man ever spoke like this man." But there is no record that anything happened *in them*. It was in those who gave themselves to him and to his way of love that the miracle of faith was wrought, so that he could say to them, "Your faith has made you well; go in peace." If our anxious, self-centered lives are to be made over—our *Angst* lifted—we too must find this healing by laying hold upon the love of God and then doing the works of love which the Christian way requires. In his will is our peace.

This is true of peace within ourselves and peace within a war-torn world. That there are political and social problems of great complexity which prevent any easy answer is clear. Yet we must not neglect the words which follow Paul's affirmation about the new creation: "God was in Christ reconciling the world to himself, not counting their trespasses against them, and entrusting to us the message of reconciliation. So we are ambassadors for Christ, God making his appeal through us." Since he has entrusted to us the message of reconciliation, must we not seek the reconciliation of men to one another and, as far as is in our power, of races to races and of nations to nations?

In the angels' chorus of the first Christmas morning we find the words,

> Glory to God in the highest,
> and on earth peace among men
> with whom he is pleased!

Are we not to suppose that God is pleased with the peacemakers? Peace on earth is the gift of God to men of goodwill; it comes permanently on no other terms. It is not given to all of us to make the hard decisions on which hang the destinies of nations; those who must make them should have our earnest prayers. It *is* given to all of us to live humbly, repentantly, in brotherly concern for all persons, and so to create that bulwark of responsible citizenship on which alone the enduring structures of peace with integrity and justice can be built.

God lives. The light still shines. Christ died in Jerusalem long ago—in that troubled Middle East —but he abides with us today in the midst of all the world's bad news. In him is God's amazing, his wonderful, gift to men, calling us to new life and to obedience in love. And if God be for us, who can be against us?

2

The Renewal of the Church

At the end of the eleventh chapter of Hebrews—that great roll call of the heroes of Old Testament faith—we find the words, "And all these, though well attested by their faith, did not receive what was promised, since God had foreseen something better for us, that apart from us they should not be made perfect." Here is stated in memorable and inspired words the ongoing movement from past to present to future in the shaping of the world through the servants of God. "That apart from us they should not be made perfect"—one could readily turn it around and expect the writer to say, "That apart from them we should not be what we are or have what we have." That would be true, and it is important. It is suggested by what immediately follows about our being "surrounded by so great a cloud of witnesses." Yet what the writer says in summation of his tribute to the past is that apart from us—the here and now of the first century and equally of the twentieth—*they* should not be made perfect. No movement is ever complete without that which lies beyond it.

It is in this mood that the church of today must adapt its message and forms of service to the needs and conditions of our time. No one needs to be told that we are living in a rapidly changing time. Populations are exploding, but so are human ideas and achievements. Old institutions crumble or swiftly take on new forms. Empires are falling, new nations emerging. Our cities and the suburbs around them continue to grow with great rapidity, and with them there is a multiplication both of new forms of comfortable living and of agonizing human problems for those unable to share in these comforts. Long-suppressed minority groups are no longer content to be second-class citizens, nor slum dwellers to accept the ghetto. The generation gap widens. New freedoms are insistently demanded. The nuclear/space age and great advances in technology have brought with them both amazing achievements and mammoth problems.

It is obvious that the churches must keep pace with such developments or become simply an archaic relic of a bygone age. So proud are we of living in the twentieth century that in some circles the way to condemn any movement or ideology is to label it "nineteenth-century." Yet certain familiar words of a nineteenth-century poet, James Russell Lowell, are so relevant to our world today that they are often quoted:

> New occasions teach new duties;
>   Time makes ancient good uncouth;
> They must upward still, and onward,
>   who would keep abreast of Truth.

In awareness of this need to bring the churches up to date we hear much today in religious talk about Dietrich Bonhoeffer and "a world come of age," about Harvey Cox and "the secular city," of the arresting if not disturbing statements of two very dynamic and outspoken bishops, Robinson in England and Pike in California, of a new reformation, a new theology, a new morality. There is talk of "holy worldliness" and of "worldly holiness," of "religionless Christianity," of the "death of God," and of Jesus as "the man for others." All these terms have arisen from the climate of thinking in which we live, and all have a meaning which requires probing before we accept or reject them wholesale. Most of them will be considered to some extent later in this book.

The net result of all this ferment is to require the churches to reexamine themselves. Some of the changes called for are definitely toward the good; about others it is harder to be enthusiastic. It is a favorite theme of the critics to say that the churches are so irrelevant, lethargic, tradition-bound, and generally ineffective that one had better leave them and get out "where the action is." This charge is leveled with special frequency against the local congregation as it conforms to the moral standards and social attitudes of the surrounding culture, and it has caused a flight by many young ministers and seminary students away from the parish ministry into other forms of service. The charge holds enough truth to prevent our being complacent about it. Yet I question that it is a fair picture of the churches as a whole.

Such critics tend to overlook the ancient, yet contemporary and precious, ministries of the church in the common ventures of life—in the Christian home and family, in times of sickness and bereavement, in times of joyous celebration, in the learning of both children and adults through the church school, in coming together weekly for public worship as part of the normal patterns of life. Granted that the church needs both to comfort and to challenge, the fact that it has sometimes comforted more and challenged less is not a sufficient reason for disparaging its ministries of comfort. Granted that the church needs mightily to serve the secular world around it, it should not be forgotten that church members are also a part of this secular world and need to find inner security and hope through the great assurances of Christian faith. Granted that worship is not all there is of Christian faith and commitment, it still remains true that it is through worship that Christians find their primary incentive and source of strength for making the world more nearly what God would have it be. Granted that Christian hope is not the only source of confident living, it is that which goes deepest and lasts longest when there are dark days and little good news in our world.

Without such ministries as these, carried on at all times and in many places and too often simply taken for granted with insufficient appreciation, both the life of the individual Christian and that of the community where he lives would be much more barren than they are.

The mainstream of the church's life goes on in the parish church and the local congregation. Were this to be abandoned, it is doubtful that much else would survive. Yet there is a place for specialized, newer forms of ministry as well. Among these are the ministry to students in university centers; various forms of chaplaincy, industrial, institutional, and academic as well as military; ministries of counseling to anxious and disordered lives; ministries in the fields of civil rights and labor relations; ministries in the leisure world, not in retirement communities only, but in the national parks, along the ski slopes, along the Las Vegas Strip, and among the hippies and the homosexuals. The French have a lovely term for what they call "ministries of presence." This means just being there and being a friend to the lonely and the friendless and those who might feel out of place in our more conventional middle-class churches.[1]

Besides these more dramatic forms of new ministry there are many others, such as urban training

[1] For an excellent survey of these new specialized ministries, see Truman Douglas, "New Forms of Ministry: Novelty or Renewal?" in *Information Service*, National Council of Churches, April 8, 1967.

centers for the inner city, literacy training centers, family service centers, suicide prevention centers. Some are sponsored by the churches, others by public agencies, but all are forms of Christian service when conducted in the spirit of Christ.

Binding all of these together are two very important developments in our time: the ministry of the laity and the ecumenical movement. In the past two decades we have been recovering something of the Reformation emphasis on the priesthood of all believers and the sacredness of the common life of work and daily activities. It would be too much to claim that laymen as a whole have begun to see themselves as the church within the world, witnessing to their faith through the activities of work, play, politics, and community relations. Yet this vital note continues to be sounded, and certainly in some measure has been heeded.

Perhaps in this brief survey of current movements for the renewal of the church, we had better put as the foremost of them all the new mood in interchurch cooperation and fellowship. Protestant efforts in this direction have been in process through much of the twentieth century, but recent developments in Roman Catholicism, and as a result between Protestants and Catholics, are the more dramatic. Renewal is what the *aggiornamento* launched by Pope John XXIII of blessed memory is all about. The four sessions of the Second Vatican Council have carried it forward with remarkable effects which have been felt in every local Catholic parish and in almost every community. Doors have been opened to an increase in fellowship and mutual understanding with Protestants, and all over the land miracles of meeting in goodwill and with common worship and study have occurred. Ecumenism is in the air, and it is one of the great forward movements for the renewal of the church in our time.

I have enumerated some of these modern movements not to suggest that all is being done that should be, but to give some evidence that we need not despair of the churches. Not enough is ever done to serve human need, and in our highly complex world with its manifold personal and social problems there will be plenty more to do until the kingdom comes!

Most of the things mentioned thus far Christians seem to approve with a fair degree of unanimity. Since these things are being done by fallible human agents, mistakes are made. Sometimes sin is discernible. There are always conservatives to be found who want no changes of any kind in the established order. Yet, on the whole, most of us would agree that these new forms of ministry ought to be engaged in, and can rejoice that churches are sponsoring and Christians are doing these things.

I turn now to four large issues in which there is far less unanimity. They will require more extended treatment later. I mention them now to suggest that any true judgment about them requires a criterion, and that criterion is to be found exactly where the author of the Letter to the Hebrews found it. These issues are the new theology, the new morality, new forms of worship, and new forms of social action.

There is no point in doing or espousing something new simply for the sake of novelty. In the field of entertainment variations are in order for novelty's sake, but this is scarcely true in religion. This is as true now as when Paul chided the Athenians for the kind of religion in which they "spent their time in nothing else, but either to tell, or to hear some new thing." New truth we must discover if we can, but it is not its novelty but its authenticity that marks it as true.

The new theology, sometimes called the radical theology, has various forms, but the one most publicized has been the "death of God" theology. It is supposed to cast off worn-out baggage and speak to the modern secular world. The churches must certainly speak to the modern world if they get a hearing, for this is the only world we have. Yet Christian faith does not stand or fall from its convergence with the prevailing mental climate of Hollywood or Harvard, of Washington or any other "secular city." If the churches were simply to echo secular thought, they would have nothing to say to the modern world that is not being said as well or better elsewhere. Our faith and our message is true or false according to its convergence with the Christian gospel—the "good news" of God—which can speak the word of renewal to every man and society. On this criterion the "death of God" theology must be found wanting.

Likewise, the new morality, which is a long way from being really new, has merit in its emphasis on the need to make all decisions in the light of the particular circumstances. It is right in making love the keynote of decision. When this is made an excuse for erotic sexual liberty, it is a sad distortion of Christian ethics and of the best secular ethics as well.

In Christian worship tradition should not prevent the introduction of new art forms. Everything traditional was once new. Is a jazz Mass or the use of folk-rock music in the liturgy introduced for the sake of attracting attention by its boldness? Such innovations are to be judged not by whether they will bring people in off the streets out of curiosity, but by whether they have reverence, dignity, and fitness to the mood of worship.

In the various fields of social action there are many complex problems for which there is no single Christian answer. Yet we do have an ultimate criterion for decision. That course of action is most nearly right which is motivated by the love commandment of Jesus when this is viewed in the light of the love of God for every man.

Neither the Bible nor the long tradition of the

church will answer every question for us in the modern world. Neither could it in days gone by, for every age is a new age in terms of its own relations with its past. This was as true of the first century as it is of the twentieth. The thrilling story in the book of Acts and the glimpses we get from Paul's letters and those of others show how the early church had to grapple with its problems as we do with ours. Yet they had one lodestone, one ultimate criterion, of what God required of them. Says the author of this Letter to the Hebrews, "Let us lay aside every weight, and sin which clings so closely, and let us run with perseverance the race that is set before us, looking to Jesus the pioneer and perfecter of our faith."

"Looking to Jesus"—that was the guideline by which they shaped their destiny. It must be ours.

Looking to Jesus, those early Christians could find common ground amid the theological tangles which were soon to disturb the church, and thus they could help to create the central stream of Christian tradition which has come down to us from the past. It is still vital today, and for want of a more precise term we call it an ecumenical theology. Its basic notes are that God lives; that this is God's world in which he calls us to work with him to make it a better world; that God is infinitely good and requires goodness in us, made as we are in his own spiritual image; that God loves and cares for all men, forgives our sin, and

36

imparts new life when we respond to his love; that in his Son Jesus Christ we see God and find both the pattern and the power for our fullest living; that as ever-present Holy Spirit, God guides and strengthens us, as he leads us forward to victorious living in this life and the next.

Looking to Jesus, those first Christians wrought out principles of right living based partly on the Ten Commandments and other teachings from their past, but uniquely also from the memory of the words and ministry of Jesus. Because of this Paul could sum up the duty of the Christian in his immortal ode to love. In a deeply troubled age, we need like our fathers to find stability in the assurance that "faith, hope, love abide, these three; but the greatest of these is love."

Looking to Jesus, those early Christians took the pattern set for them in the Jewish synagogue and made it into Christian worship. There was prayer and praise, often with reverent but joyous singing; there was reading of the Scripture; there was preaching to interpret and apply it; there was a final blessing. Through the years the forms of worship have become varied but have never strayed far from this common center. Whatever the variations, we had better not let worship get so far away from this age-old and time-tested pattern that it becomes swallowed up in entertainment.

Looking to Jesus, those men of old, whether in

New Testament times or in later years, felt called to minister in Christ's name to the sick, the poor, the ignorant, the lonely, the outcast. As a result the church was destined to build great hospitals, schools, universities, and other institutions of welfare or service to minister to human needs. Many of these services are now performed by public agencies, but we do well not to forget that it was the church that spearheaded the endeavor. Furthermore, it was the church and its gospel of the worth of every man that laid the major foundations of what was to become one of our most prized possessions—the spirit and form of democracy.

We have this heritage. We surrender it at our peril. Adapt it to the new world of the present we must. And carry it forward we must. In an ultimate sense the future of the world is in God's hands as he brings to fulfillment his long purposes. Yet in a more immediate sense it is our responsibility to carry forward what has been entrusted to us and to leave the world better than we found it. Fidelity in new duties and new tasks and faithful obedience to the call of God in old duties and tasks which are by no means outworn are required of every Christian. So, if we would be God's servants in our time and God's agents for the renewal of Christ's church, "let us lay aside every weight, and sin which clings so closely, and let us run with perseverance the race that is set before us, looking to Jesus the pioneer and perfecter of our faith."

3

The Bible—Its Message for Our Day

A story is told of the precocious son of a university professor who, having nothing better to do, spent an afternoon browsing through his father's library. At dinner that evening he reported that he had come upon a quaint and interesting book, desultory in plot, archaic in style, yet full of arresting incidents. It was called, or so he reported its title, "the Holy Bible."

I do not vouch for the truth of this story. Yet it illustrates the situation in our times. The Bible through the centuries has been the most influential book ever written, far exceeding in frequency of publication and in readership the literature of Greece and Rome, the plays of Shakespeare, or any other great literature whether ancient or modern. Yet today it is found more often on bookshelves than in the hands of readers, and among today's youth and many of their parents there is a colossal ignorance of its content.

I shall not dwell at length on the reasons for this situation, though two of them lie near the surface. One is its exclusion from the public schools in our pluralistic society, though it ought to be better known than it is that the Supreme Court, in the same decision that spoke against school prayers, clearly affirmed the legitimacy of the study of the Bible as literature and social history. The other reason for lack of general familiarity with the Bible is that in neither the church school nor the home has the Bible been given serious enough attention. And this fact points to a more basic reason. The secularization of our society has tended toward the depreciation of all things religious, and partly through lack of any compelling interest, partly through the feeling that such an archaic book can say nothing to a scientific age, the Bible has been left sitting on the library shelf.

If science is our only concern, we had better not go to the Bible expecting to be informed. It was written over a long period by many writers, from approximately a thousand years before Christ to the second century of the Christian era. None of its writers were scientists, for science as we understand it today had not yet emerged. One of the surest ways to distort the Bible is to try to make science out of it, as some literalists even in the present do who believe that creation occurred in six twenty-four-hour days, or as the explainers-of-everything do who try to get around the problem by quoting, "With the Lord one day is as a thousand years." Fortunately, we are moving away from that sort of credulity and distortion. Yet, as we reject the prescientific framework of the Bible with its "three-story universe," we too often reject with it much that is true, valuable, and very applicable to our time.

The Bible is a library of sixty-six books, and they contain many different kinds of literature: history, ancient law codes, prophecy, biography, poetry, epigrams, philosophy, drama, short stories, fables, vignettes of human frailty and divine purpose that we call parables, moral counsel, letters, sermons, memories of the past and visions of the future. Each part of the Bible is best understood according to its own nature and the authorship and circumstances of its writing, a study on which biblical scholarship for more than a hundred years has been throwing a great deal of light.

Yet through the entire Bible runs the theme of man's encounter with God. Disparate though many elements in the Bible are, as one may well expect to find them, there is still a great unity in its portrayal of the yearning love of God who endeavors to lead his people to a better life. All the way from the great hymn of creation with which the Bible opens to the "Come, Lord Jesus" with which the book of Revelation ends, this is its theme.

For scientific writing there is plenty of other literature to consult in our time. Yet science, important as it is, is not man's only interest. Among the things which modern man thinks about, though he does not always clearly put his thoughts into words, are such questions as these: Does life really make sense? Is there anything solid—any

41

ground to stand on—in this changing and often frustrating world? Who and what am I? What am I here for? Where am I going, if anywhere? Does it make any difference what I do or how I act? I want to be happy—everybody does—but how? With so much conflict and confusion in the world is there any hope for the future? How is the world going to get out of its mess? There is seldom a serious discussion today, either among thoughtful young people or their elders, in which the conversation does not eventually get around to some such questions as these. It may begin with sex or sports, cars or current happenings, or any of the trivia which so largely make up human existence. It is not likely to end there, for there are deep probings of the mind and heart to which the spirit seeks an answer.

Such questions as these are the terrain in which the Bible has a message for our day. The answers do not come neatly packaged. Even love, the keynote of the Bible's message, is a "many-splendored thing" which requires far more than superficial thought. All truth to be gleaned from the Bible must be placed in a dual setting: that in which the original writer saw it and that in which it is to be applied in the life of today. The truth must not be shifted around to suit our convenience but neither, if it is really true, should it be discarded as outworn. When the Bible is read for what it is— the record of the human spiritual pilgrimage as man meets God in the events of actual living—it is a very contemporary book.

The kind of questions just outlined and the kind of things which the Bible says in response to them are very large issues. Each requires a book in itself, and many books have been written on them. Yet with the hope of at least suggesting some of the central issues, I shall try to say something on two of them. Does life make sense? Who and what am I?

There are many people today who say that life does not make sense—that it has no meaning, purpose, or design beyond the passing pleasures of the moment. The more thoughtful hedonist would qualify this statement to add "beyond the future pleasures and satisfactions to be acquired by sensible calculation." But then come unexpected and shattering circumstances—a deep disappointment in love or in labor, the loss of a job or of money or of status, a crippling illness, the breakup of a family, the death of a loved one, some natural disaster or civil turmoil or the demands of a war to sweep away both inner and outer security—and this pleasure philosophy turns to bitterness and despair. The social result in our time is an appalling increase in mental illness, suicide, death on the highways from reckless or drunken driving, drug consumption, and crime.

The assumption that life makes no sense is widely reflected in the art forms of our time. It is reflected in raucous music, in meaningless blobs that pass as fine paintings, in sculpture that combines pieces of junk to look like nothing in particular. It is still more clearly expressed in the novels and drama of our day. Many examples could be given, but one must suffice. Samuel Beckett, who wrote the much discussed *Waiting for Godot*— the Godot who never came—has produced another book entitled *Stories and Texts for Nothing*. As the scene opens, an old man has just been thrown bodily out of the house and down the stairs, we don't know why. As he lies there in the mud, the door opens again and his hat comes sailing after him, and the door slams shut. After awhile he picks himself up, puts on the crazy old hat as if it were all he had left, and totters off, going nowhere. Such symbolic pictures of aimlessness, alienation, and estrangement have become very common in our time.

But what has the Bible to say to this frame of mind? It opens with the majestic words: "In the beginning God created the heavens and the earth. The earth was without form and void, and darkness was upon the face of the deep; and the Spirit of God was moving over the face of the waters. And God said, 'Let there be light'; and there was light." The remainder of the chapter is a hymn that tells of successive stages of creation, and after each stanza is the refrain, "And God saw that it was good."

This theme runs throughout the Bible. The Bible does not say that everything that happens is good, or that everything happens just as God desires it to occur. On the contrary man, God's supreme creation, is soon driven out of Eden for his presumptuous sinning, and the sinning is multiplied as the human family takes on the proportions of tribe and nation. As sin increases, so does suffering. Cain kills his brother Abel; the people try to erect a tower of Babel reaching up to heaven, and they are scattered abroad with the confusion of many languages. The chosen people are reduced to slavery in Egypt; they suffer many hardships as they journey toward the Promised Land; warfare with its killing and dying awaits them there. They conquer it, but internal strife develops as they wage almost continual warfare with their neighbors. After a brief but glorious united kingdom under King David, the nation falls apart; strife continues; their enemies prevail; and the ablest of the people are carried into exile in Babylon. Permitted to return by the good king Cyrus, they slowly and painfully rebuild the nation, but never to its former greatness. Eventually they fall prey to the Roman legions, and Israel as an independent and sovereign nation does not exist again until the mid-twentieth century.

But what was God doing through all this time of turmoil and strain? He kept on loving his people with whom he had made a covenant, even though he had to rebuke them again and again for breaking their side of it. God kept on guiding them, forgiving them, saving them, and all the while assuring them of his sustaining care and their own great mission and destiny. Although the covenant to be their God if they would be his obedient people was repeatedly broken, he did not abrogate it. He gave them Moses to lead them out of bondage and law codes for justice and harmony in human relations. To say that these codes emerged from the social conditions of the time, as we well may, is not to deny the work of God in their fashioning. He gave them prophets—to condemn their oppressing of one another, for the rich took unfair advantage of the poor, and the strong the weak, as men do today; to chide them for the superficiality of their religious observances when human need was left unserved; to rebuke them for following after strange gods and to call them back to faithfulness. In the highest insights of the prophets God promised to send a Messiah, a Redeemer, to save the people from their sins, and then the people who sat in darkness would see a great light.

Meanwhile, God moved the psalmists, the singers of Israel, to express this faith in immortal poetry. Here are written the sorrow, the penitence, the sense of being assailed and almost vanquished by their enemies, at times the despair of the people but at the same time an undying hope. Any number of these hymns could be cited as speaking to our day, but perhaps there is a special appropriateness in the changing moods of the forty-sixth psalm:

> God is our refuge and strength,
>   a very present help in trouble.
> Therefore we will not fear
>   though the earth should change,
>   though the mountains shake
>   in the heart of the sea;
> though its waters roar and foam,
>   though the mountains tremble
>   with its tumult.

Then God speaks to give his word of assurance amid the tumult,

> Be still, and know that I am God.
>   I am exalted among the nations,
>   I am exalted in the earth!

In the fullness of time, to borrow Paul's phrase, God sent the promised Redeemer and Savior. So, in the New Testament we have the beautiful poetic stories of his birth, which bring high art to our Christmas season; the four variant but essentially converging records of his teaching and of his ministry of counsel, compassion, and healing; his death at the hands of those who so misunderstood his message as to think him instigating treason against both the state and the religious establishment; and then the glorious hope begotten in the faithful by what happened on Easter morning. The rest of the New Testament is a fascinating account by narrative, by letter, and by apocalypse of how the church came into being through the Holy Spirit in the light of that Good Friday and Easter faith. Of this faith we are the inheritors, and if our eyes are not too veiled by other preoccupations or our hearts too dull to hear the message, that same faith can be ours today.

In this survey of the biblical answer to the question, "Does life make sense?" I have tried to let the Bible speak for itself as under particular human conditions extending over many centuries it gives a universal answer to universal human needs. Yet a further word, even though not at this point an extended one, should be said as to how current trends in theology approach this question.

There are concepts of God which are tangent to the biblical position in those types of theology now most widely being discussed. In the "death of God" theology which calls itself Christian atheism; in the widely influential theology of the late Paul Tillich which views God not as a personal being but as the Ground of all being and the object of man's ultimate concern; in the position which Bishop John A. T. Robinson calls "panentheism," God in everything but not to be viewed as a supranatural person; and in much of the secularistically oriented theology of "man come of age" which looks to

Dietrich Bonhoeffer as its chief sponsor—in all these there are attempts to establish the meaningfulness of existence on the basis of some aspects of the biblical heritage. They have done us good in challenging us to examine our own positions and make both our theology and our Christian message more relevant to the world around us than they have sometimes been. In varying degrees they speak to our age and encourage Christians to the service of the world in the spirit of loving concern. Yet I am forced to conclude that none of these approaches gives an answer to the question, "Does life make sense?" which is either as profoundly true or as pragmatically helpful as does the biblical view of a personal God which I have tried to outline. The reasons why I judge these views to be inadequate must be deferred to a fuller discussion of the new theology.

To sum up our answer to the first question, the Bible assures us that life makes sense because God is the ultimate Creator of the world, the Ground of all our existence, whose eternal purposes for good are seen in his many "mighty acts" but supremely in Jesus Christ. These purposes are being worked out amid the vicissitudes of our earthly history. We may well leave it to the natural and social sciences to describe within their own fields the ongoing processes of our existence; yet God is the source and the foundation of our faith that life is good in spite of all its turmoil. Creation is unfinished, for both human sin and natural evils are yet to be conquered, and in this God calls us to be his servants and co-workers. Nevertheless, "God the Father Almighty, maker of heaven and earth" is in final control, and with the psalmist we too can say:

> God is our refuge and strength,
> a very present help in trouble.

And with this faith, no one needs to walk off alone into the void.

We hear today quite often the phrase "a crisis of identity." This may mean a number of things, among them the sense of alienation, of loneliness, and of the meaninglessness of life. But central to it is the lack of a satisfying answer to the question, "Who am I, what am I, where am I going?" This brings us to our second major question as to the Bible's message for our day.[1]

Let us turn again to that great first chapter of Genesis. As the climax of the story of creation we read:

So God created man in his own image, in the image of God he created him; male and female he created them. And God blessed them, and God said to them, "Be

[1] The universality of this query is suggested by the fact that the artist Gauguin wrote on the margin of one of his paintings the words, "Who am I? Where did I come from? Where am I going?"

50

fruitful and multiply, and fill the earth and subdue it; and have dominion over the fish of the sea and over the birds of the air and over every living thing that moves upon the earth."

In this ancient word about fishes and birds and cattle and creeping things we have some very great words about man's relation to the resources of the earth, whether they be those mentioned or those of our day such as electricity, uranium, high explosives, metals for many kinds of machines, or the world's food supplies. The injunction to "be fruitful and multiply" is in no danger of not being heeded; there *is* danger that man in his dominion over the earth will not do what is needed to provide food for all. What the author appears to be saying is that God has given to man a delegated responsibility—a stewardship—to use his good gifts for human good as men seek to "fill the earth and subdue it." Whatever man's prowess, it is still God's world. Man is to use it as God would have it used. As man "subdues" the earth, he is to work with God to increase its good and eliminate its evils. Though our times differ greatly from those in which these words were written, they nevertheless contain an important message as to the right use of natural resources and human labor.

But let us look now at another aspect of this passage. "So God created man in his own image, in the image of God he created him; male and female

he created them." Nothing could more clearly state
the greatness and the dignity of man, and of all
persons, both male and female. We are made akin
to God in reason and intelligence, in creativity, in
capacity for giving and receiving love. In short, un-
like anything else in all creation we are moral
beings, endowed by the Creator with the capacity
of freely making moral decisions and the awful
but glorious responsibility of making the right
ones. Not alone man's technical skill in subduing
the earth, but still more vitally, his ability under
God to subdue himself and to live as one made in
God's spiritual image ought to live is what matters
most in human existence.

And how has man used this responsibility? The
mythological story of man's Fall in the third chapter of Genesis carries beneath the story the profound truth that man has defiled his divine image,
misused his freedom, and in proud yet humiliating
self-assertion tried to be God. Adam, prototype of
universal man, for this is what the word *adham*
means, might be admired for his initiative except
that, like most of us when things go wrong, he
tries to pass the buck and put the blame on somebody else. Adam blames Eve for his disobedience,
and Eve, not having any other human around to
blame, puts it on the serpent! It is not that the
knowledge of good and evil was bad in itself. This
is something we all need, and God had already
bestowed a high measure of this capacity on man

in creating him with a conscience, or there could be no sin. What was wrong was the arrogant, self-centered, and hence disobedient use of God's good gift. Here is epitomized a universal tendency of human nature, and the result is what much of the Bible and much of human history is about.

But how does God deal with sin? We have noted something of how the righteous God dealt with unrighteousness in the Old Testament, modes of tender yearning, rebuking, forgiving, and guiding that with changes in the social setting but not in human nature are still relevant today. But let us look further at the message of the New Testament.

Jesus knew as clearly as anyone who ever lived the sinfulness of the human creature that was made in God's image. There are not many more stinging words in all literature than the "Woe unto you, scribes and Pharisees, hypocrites!" with which he rebukes the double-dealing of the religious leaders of his time, although by their standards and those common enough today they were not very bad men. Their offense was that while they kept the law, they did not care about people. In the Sermon on the Mount, Jesus cut through the veneer of correct observance of the Ten Commandments to condemn such sins of the heart as anger, lust, duplicity, retaliation, and the heaping up of empty phrases in the name of religion.

Yet rebuke was not the primary way Jesus dealt with human sinfulness. In the simple but meaningful sentence, "He went about doing good," we have the key to it. There was love not only on the lips but in the life of Jesus, and he loved people out of their evil ways and into a new life in fidelity to the call of God. Eventually he died for love of God and for love of man.

Then came the Resurrection, token of God's own victory over sin and death. We cannot be sure exactly what happened on that first Easter morning, and we had better not be too dogmatic about an event of which the descriptions have an air of holy mystery as well as of glad surprise. Yet the transformation of a band of fishermen and small artisans, downcast because they thought both their leader and their cause were dead, into flaming and able witnesses for Christ is evidence enough that the Resurrection happened.

In this faith the church was born. As we read the record of courageous witness in the book of Acts, we know that the Holy Spirit had put iron into the souls of those early Christians. Human and fallible they were, like all of us, and sometimes they quarreled with each other, and occasionally they capitulated to pressure. Yet, on the whole, they were new men.

Paul in his Letter to the Galatians at one point enumerates fifteen ugly sins, common then and common now. Says he, "Now the works of the flesh are plain: immorality, impurity, licentiousness, idolatry, sorcery, enmity, strife, jealousy, anger, selfishness, dissension, party spirit, envy, drunkenness, carousing, and the like." Yet two sentences later he observes, "But the fruit of the Spirit is love, joy, peace, patience, kindness, goodness, faithfulness, gentleness, self-control; against such there is no law."

Who are we? What are we? We are made in God's own spiritual image, with a dignity and a worth above all lesser creatures. As the psalmist puts it, ranking man above all the wonders of the heavens:

Yet thou hast made him little less than God,
    and dost crown him with glory and honor.
Thou hast given him dominion over the works of
    thy hands;
    thou hast put all things under his feet.

This is our high calling and destiny. Yet every man is a sinner. If we are honest with ourselves, we must say with Paul, as he in turn echoes the word of the psalmist, "None is righteous, no, not one." Yet this is never God's last word.

What is God's word to sinning, suffering humanity in our time? It is found on many pages of the Bible, and it is a word which God speaks to every age, to our own as forcefully as to any in the past. It has been many times restated, but perhaps it was never better stated than in Paul's second letter to the Corinthian church, living as they did in a city of glittering wealth and prestige but inward shallowness. To this group of Christians he wrote:

Therefore, if any one is in Christ, he is a new creation; the old has passed away, behold, the new has come. All this is from God, who through Christ reconciled us to himself and gave us the ministry of reconciliation; . . . God was in Christ reconciling the world to himself, not counting their trespasses against them, and entrusting to us the message of reconciliation.

In these words I find summed up the Bible's message to our day.

4

Prayer and Twentieth-Century Man

H. G. Wells recounts the story of an archbishop who, feeling the need of spiritual help and guidance, went late one evening into his private chapel to pray. He knelt at the altar and began his prayer with the words, "O God." He got no further when he heard a voice which said, "Yes, what is it?" Startled, he fell over with a heart attack, and the next morning they found his lifeless body sprawled on the carpet near the steps on which he had been kneeling.[1]

The trouble with this story is, of course, that the bishop did not live to tell anybody what he had heard—so how do we know that he heard anything? Yet it illustrates well enough the incredulity of many people today as to whether anybody hears when we address God in prayer. From custom and long tradition we have not only prayers in church on Sunday morning but prayers at weddings and funerals, and we have invocations at presidential inaugurals and many other kinds of civic ceremonies. These must be carefully balanced in a pluralistic society to make sure that all the major faiths get their fair share of opportunities to be heard, by men as well as by the Almighty. We bow

[1] "Answer to Prayer," the *New Yorker*, May 1, 1937.

our heads reverently and then move on to what to many seems the real and more important business of the day.

Can prayer be made to seem a living and vital thing to twentieth-century man? Can words addressed to a supposedly real but certainly invisible Person make any difference in a day of swiftly expanding scientific knowledge, of space vehicles and computers, of political tensions and civil rights struggles? It was the poet Algernon Swinburne who in his "Hymn of Man" wrote years ago in ironic imitation of familiar words,

> Glory to Man in the highest!
> for Man is the master of things.

Whether stated or expressed, it is much in the mood of our day to assume that things and what man can do with them are what really matter, while God is a vague Something—we know not what—to be thought about, if at all, only in church and on special occasions.

Nobody knows how many people pray privately, but it is strongly to be suspected that, aside from severe crises, not many do unless we count the vague musings that go on in the minds of would-be worshipers while the minister offers the pulpit prayer. Even in this process most of us, if we were really honest, would have to confess that we often only half listen, or even fall asleep. This may be beneficial relaxation, but it is hardly prayer. As for personal or family devotions, it appears not to be a very general practice. In times of emergency or extreme danger almost everybody prays. There seems to be a deep-seated if not innate impulse to cry out for divine help when human effort seems unavailing. Yet in the ordinary run of things we tend to go about our tasks with little thought of God, whether in thanksgiving, penitence, or petition.

With many the prayer habit has lapsed through indifference or the pressure of many duties and rival claimants for attention in a busy world. There are others who do not pray because they have renounced belief in God, or at least in the kind of God who could hear and answer prayer. Some forms of worship may remain as a mood of reverence for the ultimate nature of things, but Christian prayer is a two-way communication between ourselves and the God whom Jesus came to reveal and to serve. This to some minds seems an anachronism in a scientific age and a form of incantation if it is attempted.

It must be stated, as bluntly as necessary, that unless one does believe in God, some higher power however dimly apprehended, some ground of our existence whether within or beyond us, there is nothing left to say about prayer. Prayer is not talking to ourselves; it is not simply cajoling ourselves into a better frame of mind. One may pray with some doubts as to what he believes about God and perchance find clarification in the process. If and when he has made up his mind that no God exists, the only honest thing to do is to stop praying. I do not know what the "death of God" theologians do in their private lives, but in their published writings prayer has little if any place. William Hamilton in *Radical Theology and the Death of God* quite consistently speaks with approval of the renunciation of the present institutional forms of the church with its "preaching, worship, prayer, ordination, the sacraments" when without belief in God one goes out to serve the present age.[2]

There is no way of knowing how many people have stopped praying because of intellectual rejection of belief in God. However, I do not believe this to be the major reason for the dearth of meaningful personal prayer in our time. The polls taken from time to time indicate that a high percentage of the people—well over ninety percent—say they believe in God. The percentage might be considerably lower in academic centers. The secularization of our society continues apace, but God seems not to have died except in the more sophisticated areas. Why, then, do we not pray, and pray more vitally than we do?

The answer lies partly in perennial aspects of

[2] Thomas J. J. Altizer and William Hamilton, *Radical Theology and the Death of God* (Indianapolis: Bobbs-Merrill, 1966), p. 7.

human nature, partly in current modes and conditions of living. Twentieth-century man in his basic constitution is not very different from man in any age. He loves and he hates, sometimes intensely and violently, sometimes with safeguards erected by social restraints. He is actuated by powerful impulses of sex, acquisitiveness, and the will to power. He wants prestige and status. He wants to have what he wants when he wants it, and he hates to be thwarted whether in love or war, business or politics. With one part of his nature he plays it safe, since he dislikes to stick his neck out; with another part of himself he will incur any labor, hardship, or danger to get what he desires. He has some concern for others, especially for those of his own family and immediate group, but like tribal man he often draws sharp lines between those of his own race and nation—the "in group"—and those of the "out group" who are apt to be thought of as enemies rather than as friends, or persons. He has promptings of conscience and a sense of duty, but these are easily rationalized and subdued when they conflict with self-interest or desire.

With this medley of impulses, twentieth-century man has a great deal to think about besides praying. From sheer preoccupation with such concerns as have been mentioned, prayer slips into the background even when it is not rejected. Or perhaps one feels subconsciously that he might have to change his way of living if he prayed earnestly to know and to do the will of God. Or, worse yet, one makes prayer a cover for self-interest by asking God to help him get his own way about things. Then, though not in these words, the prayer becomes in effect, "O God, I want something very badly. My will, not thine, be done!"

There are other forces besides these perennial yet contemporary aspects of human nature that set up barriers to our praying. The barriers lie partly in the conditions of our living, which do differ considerably from those of our fathers. We are "just too busy," and "we have too much to do" in a hurried and harried and complex world. As a consequence, preoccupation with other concerns replaces prayer. To be a deep-seated personal practice prayer needs to be nourished in a Christian home and in a Christian church; but competition with the claims of school, business, recreation, community interests, and multiform other activities keeps us so busy going to and fro that we have little time left to hear God speak to us and say, "Be still, and know that I am God." Even our good works tend to become activities excluding the prayer that could give them meaning and direction. Ministers of the gospel as well as lay persons fall prey to this subtle temptation.

Within such a situation twentieth-century man —and, of course, woman also—is more or less happy. I say "more or less" advisedly, for one's degree of contentment varies immensely both with his external situation and the manner in which he inwardly responds to it. Yet anxiety, loneliness, and an inner lack of peace of mind and soul lurk close to the surface, often covered with a veneer of self-sufficiency which washes away when trouble strikes. This is why we have so much frustration, confusion, and insecurity that lead to the feeling, widespread and much talked of in our time, that life makes no sense and has no meaning beyond the temporary pleasures one may wrest from it.

Within this situation it is not surprising that gigantic social problems develop. Alcoholism and drug addiction increase. Standards of marriage and family life seem less binding. Riots break forth in our cities because frustrated members of a dark-skinned race who live in ghettos are determined that deep-seated discrimination shall be challenged, if not by political and economic measures, then by violence. Crime increases until many of us who live even in cultured educational centers hesitate to be on the streets at night. War with its present potential for the destruction of all mankind becomes more frequent, and a nation which prides itself on a humane and civilized culture resorts to napalm and antipersonnel bombs to melt and maim the flesh, not only of military forces but of old men, women, and little children, as civilian villages go up in flames in the land we seek to liberate. In all this state of affairs we tend to blame somebody else instead of looking within at our own indifference and saying with the publican of old, "God, be merciful to me, a sinner."

I do not say that prayer alone would correct all these personal and social ills. It is blasphemy to make prayer a substitute for effort when constructive action is within our power. Yet humble, vital, God-centered prayer would go far toward correcting what is wrong with *us,* and there can be no reconstructed world without reconstructed persons.

So, let us turn now to what prayer is, and what may and may not be expected from it. Prayer in its essence is the humble, grateful, contrite approach of man to God, in trust of God's sustaining power and in obedience to his will. Prayer "in Christ's name" is man's self-offering before the God whom we know through Christ, with an openness of spirit to discover and do in the spirit of Christ what God would have us do.

Prayer has several essential components, though in actual praying we do not need to draw the lines too sharply between them. It begins properly in an attitude of willingness to listen as God speaks to us in the inner recesses of the human spirit. This speaking is seldom heard as an audible voice, but is more often sensed as an inward reorientation and the quieting of the claims of outward rivals. Such quieting to be at its best takes time and will-power, and this is a price we too seldom pay. Physical withdrawal from the pressure of conflicting claims is helpful, but it is not essential. In any situation, however complex, God can hear us, and we do well, like Brother Lawrence, to "practice the presence of God" not only at special times but within the duties and demands of every day.

Then, what is our part as we speak to God? If we are to include the full gamut of Christian prayer, our approach begins in adoration and praise, with which are mingled thanksgiving and gratitude. Any one of us, even in hours of darkness, can recall and thank God gratefully for our many blessings. The great words of exalted adoration fit more readily into public worship, but they can be expressed by us in the words of Scripture, if not in our own. Then since every man sins and even the best of us falls short of what we ought to be and to do, there is an important place for the mood of penitence. Petition is not all there is of prayer but it is an important part, and it is apt to be here that the more serious questions begin to arise. And the questions continue even to the point of bafflement, if not outright rejection, in the matter of prayer for others.

Let us look at each of these major components of prayer one after the other, though in actual praying they are apt to vary with the situation and require no special sequence. As we look at them, we shall also look at some of the more common questions of twentieth-century man in regard to them.

The prayer of praise and thanksgiving requires both less and more of us than any of the others. It requires more because, if it is deep and searching, it calls for breaking loose from our self-centeredness. Said the psalmist,

> I bless the Lord who gives me counsel;
>   in the night also my heart instructs me.
> I keep the Lord always before me;
>   because he is at my right hand, I shall not be moved.

To keep the Lord always before us, even though we may believe in our minds in his omnipresence, is not an easy matter. Yet, on the other hand, the prayer of adoration with its mood of humble and reverent joy before that which is far greater than ourselves is open even to the person who finds himself unable to accept belief in the personal God of biblical Christian faith. I recall a student's saying, "I just can't pray to your God. All I can do with mine is to praise it for being." In more scholarly language Albert Einstein wrote,

Whoever has undergone the intense experience of successful advances in the domain of scientific thought is moved by profound reverence for the rationality made manifest in existence. . . . [He] thereby attains a humble attitude of mind toward the grandeur of reason incarnate in existence which, in its profoundest depths, in inaccessible to man.[3]

Such an attitude of "profound reverence" is not to be disparaged. Yet one whose life and thought are oriented toward the God of biblical faith may say, further, that the very fact of "the grandeur of reason incarnate in existence" points toward the God who is supreme Mind. The emergence of new and higher forms of existence in the evolutionary process is an index of supreme purpose. The moral order of the universe, which man does not make but which he finds responding to his efforts at goodness or discovers to his sorrow by his defiance of it, bespeaks the ultimate source of all goodness. This moral order is often questioned today since evil seems so often to triumph, but this is nothing new, and in the long look history moves forward on the side of truth and goodness.

If prayer is viewed in the larger framework of the way God works with free man in an orderly world, there is no conflict between scientific truth and prayer to the personal God of Christian faith. Yet if one is unable to do more than to be humble and reverent before the mystery of the ultimate, one should do this even though it is inadequate from the standpoint of Christian prayer. Christian worship takes many forms, but it sings its faith in

[3] In a paper presented before the Conference on Science, Philosophy, and Religion.

an exultant "Glory to God in the highest" and a hallelujah chorus.

As for the prayer of personal thanksgiving, there is an old-time gospel song with too jingly a tune but true sentiment which says,

Count your many blessings, name them one by one;
And it will surprise you what the Lord has done.

Unless our mood is that of feeling that the Lord ought always to give us a smooth and easy journey through life with never a rough spot along the way, we can thank God with a glad and grateful heart for what the Prayer of General Thanksgiving calls "our creation, preservation, and all the blessings of this life."

The prayer of penitence occupies less place in contemporary than in earlier thought. It is not that we sin less, but we give more attention to the social causes and effects of evildoing, and even though we do plenty of affixing blame in human terms, we tend to recoil from the idea of divine judgment. From one angle this attention to the causes of wrong behavior is good, since it makes us more charitable and prompts us to take corrective steps. Yet, on the other hand, the tendency to regard every undesirable act not as sin but as maladjustment or mistake, the result of social conditioning or some physiological or psychological defect, has gone far toward washing out the sense of personal responsibility. Contemporary with this development, the slipping of long-established moral standards and the dissolving of all absolutes, whether of God or of a moral order, have left great numbers of persons adrift in a sea of relativity with no anchor to tie to. What wonder, then, that crimes of robbery and violence have greatly increased and sexual standards have so largely crumbled!

As a result, we need a recovery of that honest self-examination which prompted the publican to pray, "God, be merciful to me a sinner." And we need this mood in reference to our social as well as our individual sinning. We need it in reference to our sins of complacency, indifference, and inaction—long called sins of omission—as well as in regard to our overt and openly recognized sinful acts. This is true whether in matters of war, or race, or labor relations, or family life. From many illustrations which could be given I choose one from a moving article in which a father tells of the return of his son's body in a gray box after one month in Vietnam. Says he:

Who then killed my son? The Vietcong? The North Vietnamese? No, not they alone. I killed him. You killed him. False and greedy patriots killed him. Prideful and ambitious politicians killed him. The armed forces of his own nation killed him. The guilt of his death is upon us all. His blood and the blood of

11,000 is upon our heads. Each new day brings more oblong gray boxes to rest on our doorstep.[4]

Whatever the political rightness or wrongness of our involvement in Vietnam, there can be little doubt that the indifference of many of us to what Jesus called "the things that make for peace" as he looked upon Jerusalem and wept over it has brought us to this tragic situation. Add to this the complacency we too often have to the grueling poverty of millions in this and other lands and our insensitivity to the feelings of persons long deprived of their rights as free persons, and we shall have a better understanding both of the causes of turmoil in our times and of our own part in it. We had better pray for forgiveness and then, to quote other words of Jesus, "bring forth fruits meet for repentance."

In the matter of prayers of petition, there are wide variations of judgment as to what it is legitimate to pray for. There are those who take literally such words as "Whatever you ask in my name, I will do it" and "If you have faith as a grain of mustard seed, you will say to this mountain, 'Move hence to yonder place,' and it will move; and nothing will be impossible to you." As a result, they ask for many things they do not receive, and if mountains are to be moved, it is not prayer but

[4] M. Edward Clark, "Home from Vietnam: June 14, 1967," *The Christian Century*, August 23, 1967, p. 1068.

bulldozers that move them. In recoil from this situation, many others refuse to pray for anything except such subjective changes as may occur in the mind and motivation of the pray-er—courage, patience, clarity of thought, guidance in decision, resoluteness in acting for the right.

Certainly we need to pray for such qualities as these. If they are enhanced through prayer, it is a result of no small importance—enough to justify the need and the value of prayers of petition. This is doubtless the area in which most of our praying should lie. But is it the only area? I believe not. Let us look more closely at that saying of Jesus, "Whatever you ask in my name, I will do it." To pray in Christ's name is not to tack a certain formula on to the end of a prayer; it is to pray throughout to the Christlike God in the spirit of love which Christ both taught and manifested in his life. In short, it is to pray that the will of God, not our will, be done. To make it a matter of self-willed demand is to turn the meaning of these words upside down. And as for the mustard seed and the mountain, have we not learned that Jesus again and again drove home a point with a vivid figure of speech? Faith we must have, or we shall not properly use the good gifts God stands ready to impart, but faith is not credulity.

It is at this point that the older, more conservative ways of thinking and those of what is termed "the new theology" come most sharply into conflict. Here we need to safeguard what is true in each without surrendering to the extremes of either position. We hear much today of "religionless Christianity" and of "holy worldliness"—terms borrowed from Dietrich Bonhoeffer's letters from prison though often without the context in which he used them. In Bishop John A. T. Robinson's *Honest to God* and some other writings of the new theology, prayer seems not to be petition addressed to a God above and beyond us, but something to be found in any serious thought about the meaning of life or any earnest effort to help others. To such writers traditional Christian prayer seems like an evasion of our own responsible action.

It is true that prayer does not solve our problems for us and ought never to be substituted for action. Furthermore, we ought not to expect God to interrupt his orderly ways of working within his world to grant all our requests upon demand. But does this eliminate the validity of petition to the God who is above and beyond our best human effort? I think not. Not only must we ask him to give us guidance in this effort and strength for our most worthy service, but there are times when all we can do—and the most we can do—is to "rest in the Lord, and wait patiently for him."

It is obvious that not every prayer, even though uttered in the most earnest faith, is answered. Nor are we to suppose that it must be the will of God that suffering continue when we pray for its removal and seem to get no response. It is too easy an answer to the agelong problem of evil to say that unanswered prayer is always due to lack of faith or to the will of God.

Does God upset the laws of nature—the regularity of the physical order with which science deals —to give us what we ask for? I see no evidence that he does, and with his world of order the source of our security that it is, I doubt that we should want him to. But this is not to say that we understand all about how God works within his world or that we should stop praying when we do not see just how the answer is to come. It is not only natural but *right* to pray for one's loved ones, for sons on the battlefield thousands of miles away, for restoration of physical health, for safety in times of danger. It is wrong to pray and then not do the things within our power that should be done. It is wrong to pray *only* in such emergencies. It is wrong to lose faith in God when the answer we ask for does not come. But it is not wrong to pray when we feel a great sense of need. A miracle, whether wrought within or beyond the laws of nature that we understand, is something that fills us with amazing joy. God can and does work miracles of healing and deliverance, but the miracle is not something to be delivered upon demand.

This brings us to the most disputed point of all —prayer for others. Some Christians of great integrity feel that they must draw the line at this, for it seems to them to savor too much of wishful thinking and almost of incantation. But should we thus hesitate? Jesus certainly prayed for others. It is part of our total Christian impulse to want to help others in any way we can, and perhaps we are too squeamish in limiting this to overt acts and direct person-to-person communication. Even if prayer for others is effective only through their knowledge of being prayed for or through the impulse it implants in us to help them by letter, gift, or other forms of service, it is still something we ought to do. I do not myself believe that this is all there is of it, for we are bound together "in the bundle of life" and prayer in the divine wisdom may well be one of the ties that most firmly unite us. The purpose of prayer for others is not to inform God of something he does not know, but to open up channels of helpfulness that might otherwise be blocked.

While prayers for others, like other forms of petition, have no guaranteed fulfillment, it seems to have been the experience of the ages and of many individuals today that results occur which validate such prayers, though we may not understand the processes. Certain it is that if with all our hearts and lives, and not in words only or in passing moods, we prayed for "peace on earth, good will toward men" or for the breaking down of "dividing walls of hostility," we should see a better world coming into being than we now have. In any case, let us try it.

"The prayer of a righteous man has great power in its effects," says the book of James. "He prayeth best, who loveth best/All things both great and small," wrote the poet Coleridge. If righteousness and love can be joined in the prayers of twentieth-century man, miracles of inner and outward advance toward the good life for all can be brought to pass.

5

The New Theology

The most recent development in Christian thought calls itself "the radical theology." It is commonly referred to as "the new theology." Either term may be used to designate various strands of contemporary thought, of which the much publicized "death of God" theology is one. What the exponents of the radical theology are saying will presently be our subject of inquiry. Yet it cannot be properly examined or assessed unless it is seen in the perspective of backgrounds and predecessors. So, we shall begin with a rapid survey of the main movements of thought within this century. This is not merely to review past history, for all of those we shall review still survive to the present and have served in one way or another to promote the emergence of the new theology.

The twentieth century has witnessed the coming to prominence, though hardly the birth *de novo,* of six major trends in Protestant theology. The situation in Roman Catholicism is much simpler, for the magisterium has carried along the age-old conservative theology wrought out in the early centuries of the Christian era, but with recent outcroppings of more liberal views which have not been officially silenced as they once were. It will be more than enough in this survey to look at the principal trends in Protestant thought since the turn of the century.

The oldest in this succession is biblical literalism, often termed fundamentalism. Its origin cannot be dated, for the tendency to view the Scriptures as the infallible and verbally inspired Word of God has existed in the church for many centuries. Yet the name for it is not so old. Alarmed by a trend that seemed to jeopardize biblically grounded faith, its exponents published in 1910-1912 a series of twelve small volumes entitled *The Fundamentals: A Testimony of the Truth.* The name stuck. The prime "fundamental," so it seemed to its defenders, was the literal inerrancy of the Scriptures in contrast with the historical understanding of the Bible which they commonly called modernism. Other doctrines regarded as fundamental were—and are—the virgin birth of Christ, his supernatural miracles, the substitutionary atonement, Christ's physical resurrection, and his imminent, physical second coming.

The attitude of the fundamentalists has often been highly critical of those holding other views. With deep convictions on both sides conflict was inevitable. It was in the same year, 1925, that the two most famous clashes between the fundamentalists and the liberals occurred. These were the Scopes trial in Dayton, Tennessee, over the right to teach evolution in the public schools and the forced resignation of Dr. Harry Emerson Fosdick from the First Presbyterian Church of New York City, which led to the establishment of Riverside Church. Less heralded but more persistent evidences of deep division were seen in the establishment of many so-called Bible colleges, the outcropping of new denominations such as the Bible Presbyterian Church of which Carl McIntire is the best known leader, and repeated attacks on liberal ministers, their seminaries, and the National Council of Churches.

Fundamentalism is no longer in the forefront of the news. I know of no major theologian who now calls himself a fundamentalist, and heresy trials seem to be a thing of the past. Yet fundamentalism is by no means dead. Its point of view is still very much alive, not only in the conservative sects where it is still standard doctrine but in many local congregations. This is especially true among those laymen who dislike both the theological and the social views of their leaders. There appears to be plenty of money behind fundamentalism for broadcasts by radio and television.

Fundamentalism ought not to be identified with the more moderate and less polemic conservatism which has replaced it among some of its more thoughtful leaders. Of this I shall speak presently. But let us look now at what fundamentalism was fighting.

Liberal theology is generally regarded as a nineteenth-century product, both because of important biblical studies which were making a literal interpretation of the Scriptures impossible and because of its coming to terms with evolution and other emerging scientific concepts. Its main rise to prominence, however, came in the second decade of the twentieth century under fundamentalist attacks, and its influence remained dominant for three decades.

The primary note in theological liberalism was —and is—the spirit of free inquiry under the guidance of reason and experience. Basic to it, therefore, is the historical understanding of the Bible, which the liberals saw as the progressive revelation of God, disclosing himself amid the events and thought forms of Hebrew history and coming to a supreme climax in Jesus of Nazareth. Though admitting the impossibility of a complete and fully accurate record of the life, ministry, and teachings of Jesus, liberalism has given great centrality to the Jesus of history as disclosed in the Gospels. Since his central teachings were of love to God and man and the embodiment of the divine purpose in the kingdom of God, these notes have been combined in the Christian's duty to advance the coming of the kingdom on earth through the creation of a more just, loving, and humane society. From this obligation the term "building the kingdom" came into considerable vogue. Referred to as the social gospel and given theological undergirding especially in the writings of Walter Rauschenbusch, this emphasis was strongly urged in regard to war, economic oppression, and racial injustice in the period between the two world wars.

From a different though related angle, liberalism saw much validity in natural theology as centered in the revelation of God throughout his entire creation. It thus had no problem in regarding each new discovery in science as a fresh disclosure of God's ways of working within his world. Exalting the worth of human personality and regarding all men as brothers under the fatherhood of God, liberalism laid strong emphasis also on human potentialities and the need to develop these potentials through education and democracy and thus to move society forward toward a better world.

The liberalism of the decades in which it was dominant has often been charged with being too man-centered and too optimistic. It did have a high sense of man's capacities as God's supreme creation, and it rejected a literal understanding of original sin as the curse laid upon Adam. Yet it had little in common with the secular humanism of the times. Its natural theology gave vigorous battle to naturalism, as its sense of the God-given worth of every man contended against the behaviorism which tended to reduce man to a complex biological organism. It asserted both the dignity and the tragic self-centeredness of man.

By the mid-1930's a new mood was evident, first

in European thought under Karl Barth and then in American theology. This was the new orthodoxy, more correctly called neo-Reformation theology, and its ascendancy lasted well through the 1950's. Its major notes were the transcendent holiness of God; his mighty acts in revelation and redemption through Christ as these are witnessed to in the Bible; the sinfulness of man and the inability of man to direct his destiny; justification by faith alone. It agreed with liberalism in the historical approach to the Bible but not in its natural theology or its confidence in man. The social gospel was generally repudiated, but something quite like it was retained under the rubric of "the responsible society."

The kingdom of God could not be dismissed since it appears so often on the lips of Jesus. But it came to be thought of in eschatological rather than this-worldly terms, as became very evident in the long discussion of the theme "Jesus Christ—the Hope of the World" prior to the Evanston Assembly of the World Council of Churches in 1954. Personal immortality, which had been a major note in liberalism, gave way to resurrection as the more accurate biblical term for God's victory over sin and death. Even the second coming of Christ, which had been renounced by the liberals as savoring too much of premillenialism, came into good standing again in more spiritual terms.

This shift from liberalism to neo-orthodoxy was

caused in part by the fact that liberalism had tended to underemphasize sin, judgment, and divine grace. After neo-Reformation thought became dominant, many liberals were glad to add its more biblically oriented emphasis to their structure of thought. They were then often referred to as neo-liberals, though those holding this position were usually quite satisfied to be called simply liberals, or evangelical liberals when a distinction from those holding a humanistic type of liberalism was called for.

Other causes of the shift away from liberalism to neo-orthodoxy were to be found in the rise of a secular liberalism which tended to blur the lines of distinction, in the influence of a more conservative type of European thought through the ecumenical movement, in a worldwide social upheaval which challenged any optimism about man and his powers, and in the emergence of some unusually able theologians. While these differed from one another in their approach, Karl Barth and Emil Brunner in Europe and Reinhold and H. Richard Niebuhr in America wielded a powerful influence for many years.

But neo-orthodoxy was itself destined to move out of the center of the theological spectrum. Three developments arose to challenge it, and these constitute the three most recent, and even contemporary, trends in Protestant thought.

One of these trends was the emergence of a new

kind of scholarly conservatism. Theologians who had formerly defended fundamentalism against liberalism began to defend the older, long-range orthodoxy against the new. Among this group were some highly trained biblical scholars who no longer insisted on the literal inerrancy of the Bible, but who for the most part retained traditional positions in regard to doctrine. One of the ablest exponents of this position was Edward J. Carnell of Fuller Theological Seminary, until his recent too-early death. The widely circulated periodical *Christianity Today,* edited until recently by Carl Henry, is the chief popular organ of this point of view.

The second movement that began to challenge neo-orthodoxy has had greater influence among theologians. It goes by the name of existentialism, though this term covers a wide variety of types of thought, including both philosophers and theologians in its scope. Taking its origin in the 1940's from a newly discovered or rediscovered Søren Kierkegaard, it diverged both toward the brilliant atheism of Jean-Paul Sartre and Albert Camus and toward new forms of theism. Karl Jaspers, Martin Heidegger, Jacques Maritain, Nicholas Berdyaev, Martin Buber, and Paul Tillich have all been regarded as existentialist philosophers, and the last four as existentialist theologians. Karl Barth is sometimes so regarded because of his emphasis on personal decision, but his thought has little affinity with these others. Rudolf Bultmann, on the other hand, is usually classed as an existentialist theologian though his thought takes its rise not from philosophical theology but from New Testament form criticism.

What, then, is existentialism? Its central note is the human situation, viewed from all angles but primarily from the angle of man's loneliness, alienation, estrangement, and loss of a sense of life's meaning. The starting point of philosophy and theology, according to existentialism, is not rational deduction or an objective observation of the world of natural order, but man's moral and emotional life, his capacity for free decisions, and his tragic impediments to such freedom. Existentialism stresses subjectivity, experience, decision, the total life situation, not such conclusions as may be derived from either logical reason or supernatural revelation. Insofar as it is a form of theology, it centers in faith's answer to the questions posed by the human situation.

We have now traced in outline five major movements in Protestant thought and have noted that each left its influence behind it in the contemporary scene. Fundamentalism and liberalism both passed from the center of the theological stage, but there are still fundamentalists and liberals, old style and new. Both neo-orthodoxy and new expressions of the old orthodoxy have their exponents. Some of the more sophisticated religious leaders class themselves as existentialists, but for this to communicate much meaning one needs to say which existentialist he follows.

This survey has obviously not tried to cover everything in the passing theological scene. For example, during the liberal era there was the theistic naturalism of Henry Nelson Wieman, which attempted to put the thought of John Dewey and Alfred North Whitehead into a Christian setting. There is the more recent process theology, which still draws much from Whitehead. There are the variations introduced by linguistic analysis and much discussion about what is called "God talk." These we must pass over on the assumption that the dominant movements prior to the emergence of the new radicalism in theology have at least been glanced at.

We come now to the new, or radical, theology. Like its predecessors this takes various forms which as a shortcut I shall call its right-wing and left-wing forms, though these terms should be understood as having no relation to right-wing or left-wing social views. One might speak of its theistic and non-theistic, or atheistic, expressions, but this critical point becomes indistinct. The terms right-wing and left-wing when defined in terms of their exponents seem the most satisfactory designation.[1]

[1] I have taken these terms from an article by Lonnie D. Kliever entitled "Mapping the Radical Theologies" in *Religion in Life,* Spring, 1967.

The first major appearance of the new theology occurred in 1963 with the publication of Bishop Robinson's *Honest to God,* which to a phenomenal degree was discussed around the world, evoking numerous books and articles in reply. Harvey Cox's *The Secular City,* appearing in 1965, contributed much to the sociological aspects of the new emphasis. Robinson and Cox may be regarded as the most influential figures in the theistic, or right-wing, form of it. Presently a spate of articles and several books introduced the public to a still more radical, or left-wing, point of view, and this became widely publicized through articles in *Time* and other secular magazines. The principal books written by the left-wing radicals are Paul van Buren's *The Secular Meaning of the Gospel* (1963), William Hamilton's *The New Essence of Christianity* (1961), Thomas J. J. Altizer's *The Gospel of Christian Atheism* (1966), and *Radical Theology and the Death of God* (1966), issued jointly by Hamilton and Altizer. Gabriel Vahanian, author of *The Death of God* (1961), is often classed with the latter group but stands nearer to the right-wing type in an almost Barthian rejection of culture-conditioned religious caricatures of the living God.

All of these men are young, and all received their theological training when neo-orthodoxy was in the ascendancy. All are much impressed with the engulfing hold of a secular society which, though it may give lip service to Christian concepts, finds its chief guidelines in science and technology and its chief interests in areas far removed from traditional Christian faith. Yet they do not deplore this secularity; they embrace it gladly not only as an inevitable but in many respects a constructive aspect of the current scene. At the same time they are disturbed by the amount of injustice in the world, and the absence of God as a curative or protective or problem-solving agent in a deeply troubled world seems to them to call for a new approach to Christian faith.

What is the relation of this emphasis to what preceded it? What they protest as the God of the churches—the God "out there" or "up there," the God who works miracles upon demand, the God who solves our problems for us and relieves us of the necessity—is by and large the God of fundamentalism which liberalism rejected years ago and neo-orthodoxy continued to repudiate. Had a better understanding of the nature of God been more widely adopted in the churches and imparted to the laity, the radicals would now have much less to protest against.

None of the radical theologians, so far as I know, claims any affiliation with the liberalism of an earlier day, though there are notes that sound like the older liberalism in the centrality they give to Jesus, their concern for social justice, their rejection of supernaturalism as a necessary part of Chris-

tian faith, and even their optimism about the
capacity of man to remake his world. None accepts
neo-orthodoxy in its Barthian or Niebuhrian form,
though the right-wing radicals seem to be trying
to preserve some aspects of what neo-orthodoxy
stood for, and the others to replace its emphasis on
divine transcendence with an immanent God or
none. I have not found them saying much about
the new though old conservatism, but suspect they
might regard it, as many do, as a more up-to-date
type of fundamentalism. It is with existentialism
and its emphasis on the human situation that they
find the greatest affinity.

Readers of Robinson's *Honest to God* will have
discerned that he draws much of his thought from
Paul Tillich, Rudolf Bultmann, and Dietrich Bonhoeffer. These three are the most immediate and
most influential predecessors of the radical
theology.

Paul Tillich was a great Christian leader whose
thought, as he put it, was "on the boundary" between theology and philosophy, between church
and society, between religion and culture, and
many other things. I think it is not unfair to his
memory to say that he was also on the boundary
between Christian and non-Christian theology. His
idea of God, not as a personal being but as the
Ground of all being; of religion as man's ultimate
concern, whatever this may be; of the Bible as
giving symbolic but not ontological descriptions

88

of the nature of God when it speaks of God as creator, judge, redeemer, father; of Christ as the New Being giving existential answers to man's questions arising from his guilt, anxiety, and inevitable death—all this and much more is the massive thought system of a great mind and spirit. One hesitates to say that it is not Christian. Yet is it? One does not find here "the God and Father of our Lord Jesus Christ," incarnate in Jesus Christ for man's redemption. The New Being to Tillich is "Jesus as the Christ," but the new being is also the transformed life of the individual as his existential questions find religious answers through his ultimate concern. While this architectonic structure rightly commands admiration, one wonders if its wide appeal does not lie mainly in its being a man-centered rather than a God-centered answer to the human predicament.

Rudolf Bultmann's thought centers in the demythologizing of the Bible, and especially of the New Testament, through the results of form criticism. As a consequence he believes we may reject the supernatural elements of the miracle stories, presupposing as they do a God who intervenes to set aside his natural order and arising in a prescientific age. Thus far many liberal and neo-orthodox theologians have no difficulty in going along with Bultmann. The crux of dissent, however, comes at the point of his holding that we know almost nothing, and perhaps really nothing, about the Jesus of the Gospels. He does not actually deny the existence of the Jesus of history, but it is the faith of the early church, and as a result our faith, that seem important to him. In his "existential hermeneutics," revelation is not historical but eschatological. Thus, Christ is the supreme "eschatological event" which, accepted in faith, makes life meaningful. In this view the life, ministry, and teachings of Jesus can be called in question along with the miracle stories; what remains and what matters is the faith inspired in his followers and vividly evident in the early days of the church, which then placed its stamp on the tradition that has come down to us.

It is evident that both Tillich and Bultmann are existentialist theologians, for they direct much attention to the human situation and what religious faith can do to make life meaningful. It is unfair to call either of them an atheist or a humanist, for they believe in a God and deny human self-sufficiency. Yet Tillich's God as the impersonal Ground of being, or Being-itself, and Bultmann's Christ without the words and deeds of Jesus are out of accord with the mainstream of historic Christianity.

Dietrich Bonhoeffer is not easy to classify. Nearly a quarter-century after his death at the hands of a Nazi hangman, he is probably the most influential theologian alive today. His *Letters and Papers from Prison* are repeatedly quoted, and other writings of his continue to be published. To a large degree he is the mentor of the radical theologians.

Bonhoeffer's thought has two quite different but not incompatible strains. On the one hand, he was a disciple of Karl Barth and believed as intensely as any other neo-orthodox theologian in the reality of the living God of biblical faith. Had he survived without martyrdom, it is unlikely that he would have approved all that has been drawn from his letters from prison. Yet Barth and others of similar emphasis saw much that was shallow in current Christianity, and Bonhoeffer shared this mood with further strictures of his own from his experiences of the war years.

Accordingly, it is not surprising that Bonhoeffer wrote in these letters of the need of "religionless Christianity," of man "come of age" and not needing God to solve his problems, of the importance of "worldly holiness," of Jesus as "the man for others," and of love as the ground of all morality. These phrases have been echoed not only by Bishop Robinson but by many others until they have become familiar slogans. What Bonhoeffer did, without surrendering his own vital faith, was to bring together the critiques of contemporary religion that were being sounded by Barth, Tillich, and Bultmann and express these in arresting terms that were heightened by the drama of his death.

Then what happened? To put it briefly at the risk of oversimplification, the right-wing radical theologians have tried to make the Christian faith relevant to the modern secular world, borrowing freely from Tillich, Bultmann, and Bonhoeffer. What they say is not at all points traditional, but it is theistic and recognizably Christian. The left-wing, or "God is dead," theologians have seized upon the negative criticisms of their predecessors and have carried these beyond any of their forerunners.

What results is the aversion to any "God talk," which van Buren thinks must be abandoned, and the "Christian atheism" of Hamilton and Altizer. In the statements of the latter two there are inconsistencies, internally and with each other, and it is difficult to know just what they mean by saying that God is dead. It seems clear, however, that they mean more than that people today no longer believe in, or rely on, God. The note of absence, silence, "nothing there," suggests that what is being affirmed is indeed atheism, with the adjective Christian signifying only a high regard for Jesus and the service of society in the spirit of "the man for others."

This appears to be the main emphasis in the thought of Hamilton, whose theology centers in the rejection of God as any kind of problem-solver, the retention of the moral pattern of Jesus (without the God of Jesus), and a recovery of optimism through human achievement if men will stop lamenting the loss of God and put human powers to work. Altizer's thought is more subtle. While he formerly wrote that God had died in our own time, his more recent position is that the God incarnate in Jesus died when Jesus died but remained in the world as an immanent Word finding embodiment in human history. This Word incarnate in the secular stream of events has no transcendent personal existence but exists only as it finds expression in human experience. Van Buren is primarily a philosopher of the linguistic analysis type but is often classed with the "death of God" theologians. He rejects both "God talk" and God's existence, though he wishes to preserve the secular meaning of the gospel by accenting the values emanating from the story and life of Jesus.

How, then, shall we assess the radical theology? Does the profound disturbance it has caused indicate progress or retrogression? One may reply in either direction.

A constructive influence stemming from it has been its disclosure of the extent to which traditional forms of Christian thought have failed to alter the attitudes of church people. Secularism, though often denounced, has gained the mastery. This should stir us to make our faith more relevant to human need. In the thrust toward accenting love and justice in the contemporary world there is a constructive note—almost a recovery of the social gospel, though the radical theology is by no means the only Christian force that is moving in this direction.

Negatively, the "death of God" theology is essentially a form of humanism which had better not be called Christian. It has attracted few followers either among the leaders or the laity of the churches. While humanism in one form or another is apt to continue in the future as it has in the long past, it is doubtful that this particular expression of it will be more than a passing flurry. The right-wing radicals have done far more for us in fashioning a bond of connection between Christian faith and the secular world, and they merit a hearing in the mood of searching self-examination.

Both the merits and limitations of the new theology may be summed up by saying that in every form of it, its exponents have hit upon an important half-truth which has then been exaggerated to appear to be the whole truth. God is not a magnified man, manipulating the world by a crude supernaturalism, but this does not warrant rejection of the personal God of biblical faith. The Christian outlook has at times been too other-worldly, but this does not justify embracing the secular world as if this were all that matters. The message of the churches has at times been too in-grown instead of being directed to the crying social needs of humanity, but this does not justify rejecting prayer, worship, or other "means of grace."

94

It is right to emphasize man's responsible choice but not to glorify human powers to the point of self-sufficiency. It is right to be hopeful, but without faith in God hope tends to become a sentimental optimism. Finally, it is right to exalt the need of obedience to the love commandment of Jesus, but to do so without the God of Jesus is flagrant inconsistency.

It is evident that the varied theological currents outlined in this survey cannot all be true to the same extent, though there may be grains of truth in each of them. What the future holds we cannot know. What we can hope for is that each will leave its residue of truth, letting its error be corrected by the winnowing processes of time. We can contribute to this end by understanding them before accepting or rejecting them. Then in our best wisdom and with the guidance of the Holy Spirit, we ought to cling to the truth that can make us free, not only from sin, but from dogmatism and vacillation.

6

The New Morality

There are two ways to consider the new morality,
quite different though related at their roots. One
way is to look around us, read the newspaper, listen
to the news and the political comments on the
radio, turn on the television, go to the movies or
the theater, read the articles and the ads in the
magazines. This will give a picture of the society of
today. Also, if we are willing to do some recol-
lecting and self-analyzing, it is illuminating to look
back and note how much our own ideas of right
and wrong have changed over the years.

The other route is to study carefully a form of
ethical theory which goes popularly by the name of
the new morality. It lays stress on the varied situations within which human behavior takes place,
and for this reason it is called situation ethics. It is
also referred to as contextual ethics, though contextual ethics is an older and broader term.

In surveying the new morality and trying to
judge it from the angle of either current practice
or ethical theory several cautions should be borne
in mind. The first is the need of a criterion, or
possibly criteria. Otherwise, whether we like it or
not will be simply a matter of personal bias, with
our likes and dislikes lodged in the subconscious
mind—or in the viscera, if one prefers a more

physiological term. A second caution is that, try as we may, we shall not wholly divest ourselves of our presuppositions. In the quest of either truth or goodness there is no presuppositionless endeavor, and we deceive ourselves if we think we have attained to complete objectivity. And third, most forms of human behavior are neither wholly good nor wholly bad. It could hardly be otherwise in an imperfect world inhabited by imperfect finite human beings. This being so, it takes a wise person to approve or condemn with due discrimination.

Let us begin with a look at the present situation. As a criterion we shall consider the good to be what enhances human dignity and makes life richer, fuller, happier, and healthier for all persons in our society. "All persons" means not only the privileged few in middle-class American society, but the rich and the poor, persons of all races and colors, persons of all nations around the world.

Amid the changing conditions and morals of the Western world, there are elements which do not meet the standards of this criterion. Yet there are others which indicate a rising concern for human values. Examples are seen in a more intelligent and active concern for the mentally ill, the physically handicapped, the retarded child, the poor, the ill-housed, the unemployed—especially the young unemployed—the elderly. There is less prejudice than formerly against those of other races and religions, despite the fact that there is still a long way to go. There is a more international outlook than formerly and a deeper and more active yearning for peace. The provision for better educational facilities at all levels and for better health care for those unable to pay the cost of it is an amazing advance of the past twenty or thirty years. In the same period women have achieved recognition in most fields of professional employment and in public life, and while there are still barriers in the political and still more in the ecclesiastical sphere, these are in process of being overcome.

The changes thus rapidly reviewed are social changes. Yet they would not have occurred in society unless there had been prior changes in moral attitudes to sanction and to promote their occurrence. When we think, as we must, of what is wrong in our society, it does not do to forget what is right. There are many measures in process which, though not achieving perfection (few things ever do), are nevertheless moving in the right direction.

Yet after these optimistic comments, we must observe also that in many respects morals are in a bad state in our society. Perhaps dishonesty in business and corruption in public life are no more common than the acquisitive impulse has made them in all the past, but astonishing disclosures have come to the surface. More widespread, however, is the breakdown in former standards of family stability and sexual morality. One marriage in four ends in divorce in this country, in some areas one marriage in two. Divorce, though undoubtedly justified in some instances, can hardly be approved when marriage is entered into lightly, even ostensibly on a trial basis, and remarriages following divorce run to five or six in one lifetime. Adultery, though not exactly condoned, is not regarded as the immoral thing it once was. Former inhibitions among the young as to premarital sexual intercourse seem to have gone on the rocks, and in spite of easy access to "the pill" and other contraceptives, unwarranted pregnancies and "shotgun marriages" occur at every social level including the best of families.

This is not surprising, for erotic stimuli are everywhere. One does not need to be a Victorian or a so-called Puritan to regret the amount of pornography found today in current literature and drama. In its basic sexuality, as in its basic acquisitiveness and other powerful impulses, this era is probably no different from any previous one. Yet no previous age has ever equalled it in the plethora of erotic stimuli which have poured forth through the mass media in the past twenty years. This we need to remember before we judge too harshly our young people who have yielded to it.

Meanwhile, crime increases on the streets and enters our homes. Riots with violent destruction of life and property, too often eliciting counterviolence, break out in many of our cities. What looked like a most promising anti-poverty program bogs down, both from lack of funds and from lack of sensitivity to "how the other half lives." [1] At the same time we pursue a long-drawn-out war which, for the first time in our history, has such slender justification that the American people are deeply divided over it. Great numbers of church and university leaders regard it as immoral. Many others see it as futile, or worse than futile, in its awesome possibilities of enlargement. It is costing a shocking number of lives on both sides of the conflict, and one of its most serious though often unrecognized costs is the hardening of our sensibilities even to the point that we rejoice when lives are lost on the other side, forgetful of the fact that they too are our brothers, beloved of God and of family and friends. In the meantime the war is reducing to a shambles the land we seek to protect, and by its thwarting of programs of economic assistance both there and here it may even be increasing rather than weakening the power of communism. Granted that the issues are complex and that those in power have hard decisions to make, the war casts a dark cloud over our time. It is a war nobody wants, yet we seem to be caught in a net from which as a nation we are either unable or unwilling to extricate ourselves.

[1] The title of a book by Jacob Riis published in 1891. In spite of many social changes the term is still poignantly descriptive.

In view of these circumstances and others which anybody can name, the moral and social situation in America can by no stretch of imagination be regarded as being what it ought to be. In spite of progress along many lines these adverse factors are part of the moral climate of our day. Good and bad together, they make up existentially the new morality of our times.

However, in this or any other situation there must be guidelines if we are not simply to drift along as the plaything of stronger forces. So let us turn to the ethical theory which commonly goes by the name of "the new morality."

The new morality is an ambiguous term which covers numerous facets of contemporary social thinking. It is most often identified with an endorsement of the current sexual liberty, though the best thinkers of the movement have not intended this to be so central as it has become. To others it suggests the ethical correlate of the "death of God" theology with acceptance of the love commandment of Jesus without the God of Jesus. However, not all its exponents renounce belief in God. It is in line with the thought of Bishop Robinson as stated in *Honest to God* and still more clearly in *The New Reformation?* Both he and other exponents draw heavily on the words of Dietrich Bonhoeffer in his *Letters and Papers from Prison* and other writings.

In its most consistent form the new morality is

called situation ethics. Paul Lehmann and Joseph Fletcher are its primary exponents, though many others have written of it from one angle or another. In America the most influential book along this line appears to have been Fletcher's *Situation Ethics,* published in 1966. This was followed in 1967 by his *Moral Responsibility: Situation Ethics at Work.* Bishop James A. Pike, in *You and the New Morality* (1967), gives many case studies of moral decisions in which he believes neither code morality nor antinomianism, but only situation ethics, can give the right guidance.

The new morality first began to be widely discussed after a chapter bearing this title appeared in *Honest to God* in 1963. However, both the idea and the name are considerably older. Fletcher attributes the term "situational" to Pope Pius XII, as he warned Catholics against it. One suspects that were he living today, he might not wish to have fathered the term.

What is it? Attention has been centered on the sexual side of the new morality. This is not surprising because this is the most startling departure from code morality. Furthermore, from long tradition it is customary to speak of "the immoral," as in a "morals" charge against someone, as designating an aberration in sexual morals. Yet this is by no means all there is of it.

Since the new morality takes various forms, we must look for its common center. The primary ground on which it is advocated is that the morality of the past has been too legalistic; and thus an appeal to codes formulated under other quite different conditions fails to be applicable to new times. These codes may be from the Bible, or from the requirements of the church, or from inherited standards of society, or even from the law of the land, and still not be conducive to true morality. All traditional prohibitions and injunctions must be examined and if necessary set aside, and every situation must be judged in the light of its own particular circumstances.

Yet this does not mean that no guideline is left. According to the new morality all moral absolutes may be dispensed with save one, the absolute obligation to act in love. As Jesus is "the man for others," so the followers of Jesus and those outside the Christian faith are called to act in love within circumstances which vary widely from one situation to another. Hence in regard to the ancient prohibitions of the Ten Commandments, "You shall not kill; you shall not commit adultery; you shall not steal; you shall not bear false witness," their validity varies with the individual situation in which a moral decision is called for.

Situation Ethics abounds in illustrations of cases where the complexity of the situation sets these injunctions as legalistic prohibitions at variance with the demands of love in a particular situation. For example, a German woman must commit adultery with a Nazi officer if she would save the life of a loved one, and many in the underground resistance movement during the Second World War were obliged to lie to the police and falsify ration cards if they were to help the Jews to escape.[2] And if this be the case in regard to legalistic codes which claim the Word of God in the Bible as their source, it is still more obviously true of those which have their origin only in the traditional patterns and attitudes of one's surroundings. Examples of social forces to be challenged by the inclusive principle of love are race prejudice, whether or not it is incorporated into law, and a puritanical asceticism toward the enjoyment of wholesome recreation and other innocent pleasures.

The substitution of love for legalism and the particular for the general is the primary object of the new morality. It cannot be too strongly emphasized that those Christian leaders and writers on moral theory who have espoused it are not only decent, fine men themselves, but they have had no intention of throwing the doors open to unbridled liberty and debauchery of any kind in human relations. They have challenged tradition, but they have hoped to put the moral practices of our day on firmer foundations than before, and thus to help our secular society, so largely suspicious of

[2] Fletcher's second book in this field, *Moral Responsibility: Situation Ethics at Work,* gives further illustrations in many areas of current society.

Christian preachment, to more solid love-centered values.

This must be said, and at the same time it must be said that certain notes in this type of moral theory have tended in the opposite direction. These notes, both implicit in it and distorted from it, have greatly colored popular attitudes and at some points have turned it into a justification for self-indulgence and rejection of the accumulated wisdom of the human race.

These aspects of the new morality, which have tended to counterbalance its main thrust toward love for one's fellow man, may be summarized as its relativism, its contemporaneity, its secularity, and its freedom. Though they dovetail into each other, I shall try to say something about each of them separately, then pull them together.[3]

But first, let us try to suggest at least a brief answer to a very complex question: "How did we get that way? What has happened to break up the old stabilities that once seemed so firm?"

The answer must be found in both cultural and theological forces. The social changes of the twentieth century are too familiar to require much elaboration. The amazing advances in technology, the explosion of ideas as well as populations, the drawing of the world together in closer proximity

---

[3] Some portions of the ensuing analysis appeared previously in an article of mine entitled "How New Is the New Morality?" which was published in *The Pulpit,* November, 1967.

but with radical divergences of thought and opinion, the anonymity and rootlessness of people plunged rapidly into new situations without social controls to sustain them, the extravaganzas of the mass media, and the amount of sex and violence purveyed in the movies and television—all have contributed.

Yet the roots of the new morality as ethical theory must be found mainly in changing theological currents. It has a close kinship with the new theology, though it is not limited to the "death of God" type. It is clearly a protest against the legalism and often the ascetic emphases of the older fundamentalism. Like the liberalism of an earlier day, it emphasizes the need to challenge giant social evils in the spirit of Jesus, though it is less grounded in the total outlook of Jesus and has less to say of Jesus' message of the kingdom of God. Like the neo-orthodoxy of Karl Barth and Reinhold Niebuhr, the new morality inveighs against the idolatries of bourgeois society as these have invaded not only society as a whole but the churches, though it is less anchored in the God of biblical faith before whom we must have no other god. Its primary foundation is the existentialist theology of the recent past, of which Dietrich Bonhoeffer and Paul Tillich are regarded as the most prophetic voices. All this will become clearer as we look further at its chief emphases, which I have noted as its relativism, its contemporaneity, its secularity, and its freedom.

The relativism of the new morality is obvious from its main emphasis on love in the particular situation. What is not so obvious is that this one absolute when divested of other supports slips away also into the flux of relativity. Love can be made to mean almost anything by the person who wishes it not to guide but to justify his conduct. Love itself is a fluctuating and ambiguous thing unless it has deep rootage. Even what is called Christian love is undependable if it is fragmentary. To be a solid support it must include in its vision the total life and ministry, the death, resurrection, and living presence of Jesus Christ. There we see love as lived at its highest. To illustrate, some of the protests of our "hippie" subculture against the environment in which they were reared are justified. Yet their advocacy of "love" along with LSD, sexual liberty, long hair, and odd attire does not guarantee the morality of their behavior. Likewise other young people, more conventional but still too immature to distinguish between biological attraction and the kind of love that leads to an enduring marriage, are only too glad to justify forbidden conduct by citing the claims of love. As a result, the new morality to many persons connotes almost entirely a new emphasis on sexual liberty.

The contemporaneity of the new morality is presupposed in its adaptation to changing circum-

stances. This is its justification for the adjective
"new." Yet it is doubtful that it is really new. Its
ethical relativism is as old as the Greek Sophists
and the declaration of Protagoras that "man is the
measure of all things." Plato antedated it when he
observed that a physician must vary his treatment
according to the nature of the patient's illness. The
book of Ecclesiastes portrays vividly the world's
continuous cycle of change and hence the need to
do the right thing at the right time. There was as
much ethical relativism, usually called social sub-
jectivism, in the 1920's as now in the 1960's. The
same argument was advanced—morals must be
relevant to a changing society. The same objection
was offered—there must be some fixed point of
reference amid the flux of social change if any act
or attitude is to be considered either good or evil.
In the days when the social gospel was a widely
accepted adjunct of liberal theology much emphasis was laid on doing in every situation, public
or private, what love demands.

We certainly ought not to quarrel with the need
to express love in a relevant way within the conditions of our time. To do so is Christian. Yet
there are other aspects of the emphasis on the new
and the immediate about which we need to be
cautious. We had better not cast aside too readily
the inherited wisdom of the past, whether
grounded in the Bible or in the conscientious feelings of mankind through the centuries. Granted

that complete unanimity in moral standards is impossible, and probably undesirable from the standpoint of human initiative if we could have it, nevertheless the safeguards of human life, family life, personal property, and personal integrity which are recorded in the Bible and have come down to us through many channels had better not be lightly disregarded. "You shall not kill"—human life; "You shall not commit adultery"—family life; "You shall not steal"—personal property; "You shall not bear false witness"—personal integrity, are to be found not only engraven on tablets of stone and recorded in the pages of a sacred book, but deeply embedded in human experience and human history.

But what of the new morality and its secularity? Under the lead of such influential figures as Friedrich Gogarten in Germany and Harvey Cox in America, much is being said about secularity as an aspect of modern life to be embraced, even though secularism may need to be challenged. Secularity is generally taken to mean the vast advances in technology and other forms of progress in today's world, while secularism connotes a widespread reliance on and concern for human interests and achievements, regardless of religious faith. The new morality, at least in its more popular forms, seems a little uncertain whether to derive its perspectives from secularism and thus conform to the world or to try to transform the world by the application of the love principle to its secularity.

A prevalent note in the churches today is the lifting up of the secular world as the dominant sphere in which to find God and to work with God to make this a better world. At this point the new morality, even where it does not go along with the "death of God" movement in its renunciation of the present institutional forms of the church, nevertheless issues a call to leave the churches with their stuffiness and middle-class morals and get out into the world "where the action is."

This may or may not mean a physical withdrawal from the membership or the leadership of the existing churches. What it does is to stress the need of the churches to take their cues from the modern world. "Modern man," a term much used in the literature of the movement, is viewed as being so completely secular in his orientation that the churches can say nothing to him except from within this perspective. Since modern man has no use for ancient dogmas or traditional moral platitudes, the secular world must be the Christian's primary standing ground and place of service. As a result, it is not surprising that many of the seminary students and the younger clergy have left the parish ministry for other forms of service.

This viewpoint is an important and a dangerous half-truth. It is, of course, true that for the church to communicate with the modern world it must come within speaking distance of it and that to serve the modern world it must minister to real needs, not imagined or outmoded ones. Yet modern man is not so homogenous as is often assumed, and every man has persistent spiritual needs, perhaps unrealized and often unconfessed, which are much the same from age to age. It is not easy to communicate the Christian gospel or the major notes of the Christian faith, of which the churches have long been the custodians, to a skeptical generation. But was it ever? There have been fluctuations in receptivity, but I know of no period when the communication of the gospel in its depths of meaning was a simple or easy process.

A basic reason why the appeal to secularity must be questioned is that both truth and love require foundations beyond the passing scene with its flux of interests. *There is nothing to say to the secular world except to echo its own assertions unless one has a perspective from beyond it.* Simply to reaffirm its assumptions and reinforce its values, even if this is done in the name of morality and religion, is not a laudable service but a pitiful surrender. Paul uttered deep wisdom when he wrote, "Do not be conformed to this world but be transformed by the renewal of your mind, that you may prove what is the will of God, what is good and acceptable and perfect."

The freedom which the new morality both promises and enjoins ought to be responsible freedom. This is the main theme of Harvey Cox's recent book, *On Not Leaving It to the Snake*. Yet the freedom advocated by defenders of the new morality is not all of one kind. At its best, it is in keeping with "the liberty of the Christian man" extolled by Luther and with Paul's declaration in Galatians 5:1, "For freedom Christ has set us free." The placing of love above the Mosaic law has high authority in the repeated affirmation of Jesus in the Sermon on the Mount, "You have heard that it was said to the men of old . . . but I say to you. . . ." At its worst—and unfortunately it is often taken at its worst—it justifies the dismissal of former sexual restraints as worn-out baggage, provided "love" is present in illicit unions. At its best it undergirds the kind of civil disobedience in defense of justice that can lead to martyrdom; at its worst it becomes an excuse for anarchy and a defiance of all the stable institutions of society.

Perhaps we are ready now to come to some inclusive assessment of the new morality.

Its primary emphasis, which hinges on the wisdom epitomized in the adage "circumstances alter cases," is not new and it is very valuable. It is to be found not only in Jesus' words in the Sermon on the Mount but in his indictment of the hypocrisy of the Pharisees because they had observed the letter of the law but had "neglected the weightier matters of the law, justice and mercy and faith." He put persons above traditional precepts when he declared that the sabbath is made for man and not man for the sabbath. The prophets repeatedly defied tradition at what they believed to be the call of God, and the early church again and again practiced civil disobedience.

The need to consider the particular situation in applying any general principle has long been accepted policy in Christian ethics. I do not know of any outstanding Protestant writer in the twentieth century who has questioned it or who has advocated an inflexible legalism. Much of the emphasis of the earlier social gospel, as well as that of the social action of today, has centered in the need to consider all persons as persons regardless of race, color, age, sex, national origin, or economic status, and to treat all in the most loving way possible under their circumstances.

Yet in this former emphasis there were safeguards—the long look both to the past and the future and the broad look toward the widest possible survey of probable consequences. I find these safeguards understressed and too often lacking in the new morality. This tends to vitiate the value of its emphasis on the contemporary situation. Let us look at a few examples from our complex contemporary scene which illustrate the need of the long look and the broad look.

While the more informed exponents of the new morality would not think of giving a wholesale sanction to adultery or extramarital sex, they leave the door open by suggesting that there might be cases where this would be right. If the wider and longer consequences both for the couple in question and society as a whole are taken into account, it is doubtful that this can properly be said. Already the adverse effects of its being said are evident in widespread unhappiness resulting from the quest for untrammeled pleasure.

From another angle, the Christian pacifist is often charged with an absolutism irrelevant to circumstances. It might be truer to say that he *does* look at the circumstances and finds war—all war—to be so destructive as to call for a different course. The nonpacifist Christian reads differently the demands of his day, but neither point of view if taken seriously is blind to the circumstances or gives a blanket sanction to war.

In the present Vietnam situation it is not a case of pacifism or nonpacifism, for great numbers of those who oppose it, including leading theologians, Protestant, Catholic, and Jewish, supported the Second World War and would again under similar circumstances. Opposition, to be justified, hinges on a realistic appraisal of the situation with the conclusion that the best interests of Vietnam, our country, and the world of nations are being thwarted rather than served by it.

The call of the Christian under some circumstances to engage in civil disobedience is by no means new. The church was born in this atmosphere, and the word of Peter to the Jerusalem

Council, "We must obey God rather than men," has long been a Christian watchword. But such action is to be engaged in only after a careful and prayerful survey of all the factors in the situation, including especially the consequences. Dietrich Bonhoeffer's decision to participate in the abortive plot to take the life of Hitler, which led to his martyrdom, is a case in point. It was an act contrary to an absolutist interpretation of the injunction, "Thou shalt not kill," and he knew well that it could only be considered an act of treason by the Nazi state. Yet he judged that the highest good of his country required it, and he made the fateful decision.

That civil disobedience is justified in some circumstances does not justify rioting in the streets, the destruction of life and property, or a defiance of civil law and order. Yet, neither is there justification for lethargy before racial discrimination, or for the indifference of the comfortably well-off Christian to the poverty, unemployment, and ghetto-type living of great masses of our fellow citizens and brothers in a common humanity. There is no easy solution of society's major problems, but only the determined, wise, and persistent application to every tangled situation of the Christian principles of love, justice, and respect for human worth and dignity can bring about any solution.

There are Christians today who base their

morals largely on legalistic codes. There are many persons, both in and outside the churches, who derive their moral judgments much more from the surrounding culture than from the love commandment of Jesus. To such persons the emphases of the new morality may come as a creative jolt. But let us not surrender too quickly our inherited anchors as we seek to serve the present age.

We cannot live in the past. Yet neither can we live effectively, serviceably, and joyfully in the present without an understanding of, and a deep respect for, the accumulated wisdom of the past. This holds true both of the biblical faith of the churches and the long-range moral standards of society. It is dangerous business to reject these simply on the ground that we live in a new age. In large part they emerged from human living, and in new forms of application human living still has need of them.

Love must indeed be our ultimate criterion. But is love all we need? Said Paul, "Faith, hope, love abide, these three; but the greatest of these is love." Our hearts respond to the wisdom of these words. But will faith and hope survive on love alone? And can human love be at its best without the undergirding of a love that is more than human? These are the crucial questions of our time.

7

The Church and the World

Throughout the earlier chapters of this book attention has been drawn to the tendency of critics of
the churches to condemn them as tradition-bound
and culture-conditioned, and to point outward
from the churches to the world as the true locus of
Christian endeavor. The critics inveigh against the
institutional aspects of the church as being too in-
grown and status-centered, against ministers for
preaching dull and platitudinous sermons, against
congregations for preferring that kind of leadership to any that might stir them to action in behalf
of human need. With the charge that the churches
lag behind other agencies in combating racial prejudice and in support of the status quo in economics and politics, there is frequently linked a
disparagement of the Bible and of the creeds of the
church as sources of truth because they are products of a prescientific age. As suggested earlier,
the churches are often charged with being too
legalistic and ascetic in their moral standards, with
an accompanying self-righteousness that, on the
one hand, quenches the impulse to Christian love
and, on the other, puts barriers in the way of
legitimate pleasures.

While there is general agreement among the

more thoughtful observers that there is some validity in these charges—enough to make it impossible to dismiss them as unwarranted gripes—there is no agreement as to the extent to which these charges are true or on what to do about them. Some want to abandon the church for other fields of interest or action; others call for its renewal (in reality, its remaking) into closer conformity with both the modern mood and the basic moral imperatives of the Christian gospel. Thus we hear a great deal today both from within and outside the churches about church renewal, new theology, new morality, new forms of ministry to the world, new breeds of clergyman, new laymen, new organizational structures, and new approaches to great social issues like those of race, poverty, war, and civil disobedience.

The issue boils down to the question of the right relationship of the church to what both the Bible and modern diction call "the world," though obviously this term connotes a vast range of objects and issues undreamed of in Bible times. In short, it is a matter of the relation of the churches to secularism, or to secularity if a distinction is drawn between these terms.

The dictionary definition of the adjective "secular" has some interesting theological connotations. It is defined as "pertaining to this world or the present life, as opposed to eternity and the life to come; having reference to temporal rather than spiritual or religious affairs; worldly." About the first item I shall make some comments later; the second comes closest to the meaning in which the term is currently used. The secular is anything not specifically religious, as becomes immediately evident when one speaks of a secular state or a secular system of public education. The term as such is neither pejorative nor laudatory; it is simply descriptive of the fact there are other institutions in society besides religious ones. Yet if, as the Christian believes, God is the Lord of all the earth and has bidden us to serve him in all the relationships of life, it at once becomes apparent that the church is inextricably bound up with the world. But how? Should the existing lines between the secular and the religious be more tightly drawn? Or are barriers erected in the past now in need of being overcome? Or must both procedures be taken simultaneously? These are questions of no small importance.

The right relation of the churches to the world, though an age-old question, has recently assumed fresh prominence. Much is being written and spoken today on both secularism and secularity, sometimes with a distinction between these terms, sometimes with no appreciable difference or with the difference if any blurred by the fact that *secular* is used with both. To trace and evaluate this literature, as John Macquarrie has done ad-

mirably in his *God and Secularity*,[1] would carry
the discussion beyond the purposes of this chapter.
But let us see if we can arrive at some of the more
viable meanings of the terms.

Of the two, secularism is the easier to define and,
at least in its more extreme forms, is more clearly
at variance with the Christian gospel. So let us
begin with this term. In my book *The Modern
Rival of Christian Faith,* which was published in
1952 with the subtitle "An Analysis of Secularism,"
I defined it as "the organization of life as if God
did not exist."[2] I see no good reason to modify
this definition, though subsequent discussion has
raised fresh issues to be considered.

To say that secularism is the organization of life
as if God did not exist is not to say that all secularists are atheists. Some are, some are not—and this
applies both to philosophers and theologians who
discuss the issue theoretically and to the ordinary
man in the street and in the church pew. The
crux of the matter, whatever one's degree of intellectual penetration, is that belief in God even
when accepted in one's mind makes to the secularist no significant difference in his living. Value
judgments, moral decisions, primary interests,
causes to support, and all that is most basic to
living is determined by social pressures and per-

---

[1] (Philadelphia: The Westminster Press, 1967.)

[2] (Nashville: Abingdon Press, 1952), pp. 11-17. The book was
written before its theme became a matter of general interest
and is now out of print.

sonal preferences regardless of professed religious beliefs. In short, it is the contemporary world rather than God that matters most.

Secularism (from *saecula,* an age or period) means concession to the spirit of the age in which one lives. Since every period has its prevailing *Zeitgeist* with its own combination of enticing objects and forces, and thus its dominant interests which fall short of being fully Christian, secularism is no new phenomenon in Christian history. Neither the medieval "age of faith," nor the puritanism of our founding fathers, nor the day of the great religious revivals, nor any scene of simple evangelical piety, nor the various prior currents of the twentieth century have ever been free from conflict and rivalry with the basic claims of the Christian gospel. Secularism in its simplest terms means the impact of the world on Christian experience, and it is unlikely that "the care of the world" will ever cease to beset the path of the Christian while sinful and fallible humanity exists upon this planet.

Our own time with its vast output of scientific knowledge and technological products, with rapid social change going on virtually everywhere, is the most complex that has appeared in all of human history. Yet this is not to say that it is the best or the worst. There is much that is good in it in spite of its darker elements of loneliness, lovelessness, insecurity, injustice, violence, cruelty, and complacent indifference to vast areas of human need. Some of these features which give us cheer were enumerated in the discussion of the new morality, and in my book on secularism to which reference has been made an entire chapter is devoted to an affirmative answer to the question, "What is right with modern life?" Yet this does not alter the fact that secularism is a major rival of Christian faith.

Secularism is by no means limited to spheres outside the churches; it is deeply embedded in them. At this point it is necessary to emphasize that one does not need to be an atheist in order to be a secularist. The polls taken intermittently continue to show that most Americans today, whether or not they are connected with churches, say that they believe in God. Although many of these persons might have trouble to define in very precise terms the nature of the God they believe in, their belief has been at least partly shaped by the Bible and our Christian heritage. I am sure that most people of any intelligence have long since renounced, if they ever held it, Pierre Berton's caricature in *The Comfortable Pew* of belief in God as "the concept of a white-bearded Big Daddy perched on a cloud" or "the Mysterious Friendly Spirit somewhere 'out there' in space." [3] The critics seem to me to have greatly overestimated modern man's renunciation of belief in God as the

[3] (Philadelphia: Lippincott, 1965), p. 106.

creator of the universe who is linked with human well-being and destiny. Nevertheless, those who believe in God "with the top of their minds," as John Baillie put it years ago, often fail to believe in him "in the bottom of their hearts." [4] As a result, secularism reigns, whether within or outside of churches.

If it is to be asserted that secularism is a serious rival of the Christian faith and the Christian gospel, reasons should be given. The first of these is the idolatry which it embodies. If there were not so many good things in the world of today, there would not be so much to compete with concern for God, or the worship of God, or the moral demands of God for service in love to one's fellowmen. Secularism is, for the most part, the quest for attractive, apparently rewarding values which become idols when they dominate the human spirit to become the arbiters of self-orientation and moral decision. Nobody in his right mind would want to dispense with these values; rather, we ought to thank God for them. Yet secularism is the more subtle rival to Christianity because to so great a degree it sets before man not bad but good ends as the goal of his effort. Conventional moral decency with some touches of an altruistic humanism then passes as Christian living. Secularism is present in churches wherever either clergy or laity

[4] *Our Knowledge of God* (New York: Scribner's, 1939), p. 52.

live by the standards of the surrounding culture instead of by the demands of the Christian gospel, and this is to say that it is present in most, if not all, churches.

A second reason why secularism runs counter to the Christian gospel is its implicit hedonism. This is not always apparent on the surface for reasons stated in the preceding paragraph. The pleasure or happiness it encourages may be sought on a low level or high, on a crudely egoistic or (within limits) an altruistic framework. There is much in our modern society that genuinely contributes to health, enlightenment, wholesome appreciations, and the improvement of society as well as one's self. Books, magazines, movies, radio, television, symphonies, sports, clubs of one kind or another, good schools, good clothes, good foods, good houses and automobiles, and in conjunction with all of these, good family life, good jobs, and good community relations are important assets of the secular world which certainly ought not to be decried. They are compatible with Christian living and should be made available to many more people than now possess them. Therefore, I do not say that the effort to secure them for one's self or for others is necessarily hedonistic. But why are these things sought? If the motivation is primarily a matter of personal comfort, prestige and status, self-satisfaction, and conformity to prevailing patterns, it still falls short of the demands of the Christian gospel and the injunction to "seek first the kingdom of God."

On the more obvious levels of self-indulgence for the sake of pleasure, as in sex, drink, drugs, and their common accompaniments in our time, the hedonism shifts to another angle. The people in the churches are prone to condemn such indulgences as immoral and then to be charged with a puritanical asceticism and pharisaic hypocrisy when they do. There is no need to repeat here what was said on these matters in the chapter on the new morality. Perhaps it is sufficient to point out that in both the indulgence and the protest, secularism reigns and invades the churches.

A third reason why secularism is a serious rival of Christian faith is its dependence on science as the final source of authority in what may be believed. It has long been established in Christian thought by all but the most conservative biblical literalists that there is no necessary conflict between scientific truth and Christian faith, provided the discoveries in science are seen as fresh disclosures of the manner in which the Creator has fashioned his world. However, when scientific knowledge is made the only dependable approach to truth, and the Bible is decried for its primitive "three-story universe" with no grasp of its enduring message, and God as the transcendent Creator above and beyond all his works is replaced by a humanly experienced "dimension of depth," as is often found in contemporary expositions of the

new theology, then a legitimate and valid respect
for science has passed over into scientism. If faith
in the God of the Bible and our Christian heritage
then survives at all, it is on one or the other of two
procedures. It is either through neglect of the inconsistencies involved in this stance or by the
twisting of historic Christianity into something
that might better be called an ethical humanism.
Both procedures, and in the more radical forms of
the new theology both in conjunction, are to be
found in current writing.

A fourth characteristic of secularism is sometimes overtly proclaimed by its exponents, perhaps
more often proclaimed by silence. As was suggested
in the dictionary definition quoted earlier, secularism is a this-worldly outlook on human existence
with nothing to say about life after death unless to
deny it outright. This is a consistent conclusion
from its scientism. While science can neither affirm
nor deny a sphere of existence which lies beyond
its scope, if science is the *only* source of knowledge
or of legitimate faith, then no ground is left for the
Christian assurance of eternal life. Some exponents
of the secularist point of view regard this dismissal
of the hope of life after death as a great gain, since
traditionally the churches have been too other-
worldly. Others believe they speak more effectively
to the modern world if they stop affirming a faith
that can have no empirical verification but put the
emphasis instead on the possibilities of progress

here on earth through human initiative and effort.

In view of these factors secularism, in spite of all that is good in its attention to the world around us, remains a rival to historic Christian faith. But do we escape from these conclusions by espousing not secularism but secularity?

"Secularity" is a term that has come into common usage to cover situations where the adjective *secular* is not a sufficient designation. It appears more frequently in current writing than the older term. One reason for its emergence appears to be that secularism has incurred an unfavorable connotation in popular diction and it is hoped that secularity as a fresher term may escape some of this odium. Yet if it is made to mean the same thing, as it often is, one wonders if a change in terminology can change the situation.

Another reason for the use of the term needs to be taken more seriously. Secularity, after all, can mean something that secularism does not.

As was indicated earlier, there are some writers, notably the late Friedrich Gogarten in Germany and Harvey Cox in America, who do not go along with the abandonment of historic biblical faith which is the end product of secularism. Rather, they see in the secularity of the modern world something to be rejoiced in as an amplification of the biblical message and to be gladly embraced by the churches. This secularity, manifest in the technological achievements and vast expansions of human power and knowledge in our time, is linked with the biblical doctrine of creation and viewed as a call to responsible stewardship.

In this understanding of secularity there are values both in its appreciation of the goodness of the world in which our lives are set and in its challenge to the people of the churches to correct the elements of misery and injustice. Certainly in the present-day world there are great expressions of creativity, human and divine, which ought to be rejoiced in. Among these are obviously not only the production of many kinds of goods to serve human needs but advances in communication and internationalization, in education as a basic concern at many levels, in provision for health and welfare among the formerly neglected, in a growing sense of the equality of all persons and the need to secure economic and political justice for all. In spite of all that clearly makes this "a time of troubles," to borrow Toynbee's phrase, these other aspects of our world are unmistakably present. If the emphasis on secularity can give us hope by directing attention to the goodness of God's world and its high potentialities, then let us rejoice in it.

Yet it will not do to turn dull or sightless eyes to the enormity of evil in today's world—evil for which men are largely responsible either through "man's inhumanity to man" or through the complacency and indifference of the comfortable to the misery of the underprivileged and the dispossessed.

The critics are right that the churches have done this to an appalling degree, though usually without intending to do so.

Many of the criticisms, as, for example, those in *The Comfortable Pew,* give a one-sided account of the situation by failing to appreciate the real and the extensive efforts that have been made. For the most part, the denominational leaders and those who head the major ecumenical bodies are concerned, not solely with the preservation of the institutions as is often charged, but with a many-sided ministry to human beings. It is the fashion today to disparage resolutions. Yet they are drafted and adopted to give guidance. Time after time, excellent statements call on both the churches and the agencies of government to support civil rights and other forms of racial justice; to counter reliance on the destructiveness of war, as in Vietnam, with more positive steps; to give support to the United Nations; to work toward better and more equitable systems of education, job opportunities, and housing for minority groups and especially the poor among them—in short, to support the steps that must be taken to eliminate the glaring evils of today's world. Such expressions of position on the part of the leadership of the churches are of no small importance.

Why, then, are not the churches more effective? No single answer can be given, but it is not all due to the indifference and tradition-bound lethargy which the critics charge. Such concerned attitudes as have been indicated on social issues are to a considerable degree shared by the clergy. Yet often the clergy do not speak out their full convictions, for if they are to have pulpits from which to speak at all, they feel that they cannot push too far ahead of those in the pews to whom they speak. So the guidelines from the higher echelons fail to filter to the pews or, if they do, are met with opposition and threatenings of withdrawal of support, whether financial or personal. The laymen in local congregations are, for the most part, well-intentioned persons and often good Christians in many aspects of their living, yet they do not want to see any major disturbance in the status quo. Such conformity is where the pull of secularism comes into the picture, and it is this more than any other force that causes churches so often to lag behind other agencies in greatly needed social change, while the excellent pronouncements go unfulfilled.

It can hardly be overemphasized that it is the tendency to conform to the standards and attitudes of the prevailing culture, whether in clergy or laity, that is chiefly responsible for the failure of the churches to speak with a more prophetic voice. Paul saw this long ago and warned against it when he wrote: "Do not be conformed to this world but be transformed by the renewal of your mind, that you may prove what is the will of God, what is good and acceptable and perfect." To be "transformed by the renewal of your mind" is to take the Christian gospel seriously. It is to be so motivated and sustained by the will and the power of God that Christians will speak to be heard on controversial issues. It means being willing to suffer to purge society of injustice—to live and, if need be, to die that the right may prevail in human relations. But in how many of us is this more than a passing admiration of the occasional few who demonstrate such a transformation?

More than a century ago Emerson in his famous essay on "Self-Reliance" wrote, "Whoso would be a man must be a nonconformist." This does not mean nonconformity for its own sake. Neither personal exhibitionism nor defiance of the moral patterns wrought out over the long past to stabilize society will enhance true manhood. Yet the Christian in obedience to the will of God and for the love of humanity must at points be a nonconformist, and take the consequences.

Seldom has the conscience of America been so stirred and called to self-examination as by the assassination of Martin Luther King, Jr. The mourning of many millions was a spontaneous response not only to a man of great courage but to a man of great faith who took seriously the call to Christian nonconformity. We do well to hear him:

"Do not conform" is difficult advice in a generation when crowd pressures have unconsciously conditioned our minds and feet to move to the rhythmic drumbeat of the status quo. Many voices and forces urge us to choose the path of least resistance, and bid us never to fight for an unpopular cause and never to be found in a pathetic minority of two or three.

Even certain of our intellectual disciplines persuade us of the need to conform. Some philosophical sociologists suggest that morality is merely group consensus and that the folkways are the right ways. Some psychologists say that mental and emotional adjustment is the reward of thinking and acting like other people.

Success, recognition, and conformity are the bywords of the modern world where everyone seems to crave the anesthetizing security of being identified with the majority. . . .

We must, of course, be well-adjusted if we are to avoid neurotic and schizophrenic personalities, but there are some things in our world to which men of goodwill must be maladjusted. I confess that I never intend to become adjusted to the evils of segregation and the crippling effects of discrimination, to the moral degeneracy of religious bigotry and the corroding effects of narrow sectarianism, to economic conditions that deprive men of work and food, and to the insanities of militarism and the self-defeating effects of physical violence.[5]

What, then, is the relation of this spirit to the old yet new emphasis on the world as the rightful sphere of the church's activity in the service of

[5] *Strength to Love* (New York: Harper & Row, 1963), pp. 8, 14.

human need? And where does secularity stand in the picture?

If the emphasis on secularity can be made to permeate both pulpit and pew to the point of wise, courageous, and Christian social action, we may well rejoice in it. Yet in the abundant literature being written on the renewal of the church, little distinction seems to be drawn between secularism and secularity. With some exceptions, the tendency is to chide the church for inaction instead of emphasizing the deep rootage in responsible stewardship and in Christian faith which its service to the world must have. Granted that it is possible to speak of secularity without the negative connotations of secularism, the distinction needs to be more sharply defined than we usually find it to be.[6] Otherwise the pull of the world upon the churches is at the same time deplored and lauded. If this is not to be sheer inconsistency we must still ask the questions, "In what respects?" and "Upon what foundations?"

So, why not say without circumlocution that secularism is at variance with the imperatives and insights of the Christian gospel, that much but by no means everything in the secular world is good, and that God calls his servants to use their utmost effort to make it a better world? We shall transform

[6] Macquarrie says of the terms, "The distinction is, perhaps, a somewhat artificial one, and I doubt if it is found outside the writings of a few contemporary theologians." *God and Secularity,* p. 20.

the world not by conforming to it, but by fidelity to a higher vision and a higher Power. The prime necessity in relation to the world around us is to be immensely concerned about it, appreciating its goodness with thanksgiving to God, deploring its evils with a resolute challenge to them in the name and the power of God, all the while keeping our own sights clear by the light from God which has come to us in Jesus Christ.

If we are willing to take these steps with courage, with love, with sensitivity to the feelings of others, and with such wisdom as we can muster under the guidance and strengthening of the Holy Spirit, *every Christian,* however humble his circumstances, can make some contribution to the good of the world. Not all such contributions will receive the acclaim of the world, and many will meet with misunderstanding and opprobrium, for the Christian gospel has a cross at its center. Nevertheless, every Christian in a reborn church can help to bring our world closer to the reign of God for which we pray each time that we repeat the prayer our Lord has taught us. And if we will do this, we shall both discover and help to ensure stability amid the awesome changes of our world.

8

Toward a Theology of Social Change

Nothing is more evident today than the rapidity of social change, both in America and around the world. There are plenty of people now living who can remember seeing their first airplane, and some their first automobile. Television and the transistor radio, now so much taken for granted, are actually only a few years old. Such developments are both symptomatic of great changes in social structures and instrumental to them.

In the less developed portions of the world, these commonplace adjuncts of contemporary living are less common, though there are few areas of the earth's surface where they are not to be found. The knowledge that these and a vast number of other products of the technological age, including more and better food, housing, and "health, education, and welfare" could be had if the economic resources were available, has stirred a deep unrest. With this has gone a deep and insistent demand for political expression and self-determination. The cry for bread, freedom, and the dignity that belongs to personhood is in the air.

With these factors pervasive in today's world, it is not surprising that revolution of one kind and another is equally pervasive. Nor is it surprising that in the demand for legitimate rights by some and the determination by others to maintain the status quo there should be conflicts and violence.

It is not my purpose to delineate in any detail these rapid social changes and resulting conflicts. The general outlines are familiar to all, and any precise description would require more technical competence in this field than I possess. My concern is with the principles of Christian social ethics that relate to procedures for dealing with them, which to be valid must be undergirded by a true and relevant theology.

The Apostles' Creed, repeated times without number throughout the centuries, is by no means a complete statement of Christian faith. Some of the phrases in it, such as our Lord's coming again "to judge the quick and the dead" and "the resurrection of the body," do not gear in well with current thinking and require considerable interpretation to be made meaningful and persuasive. The phrase "born of the Virgin Mary," taken too often as the major criterion for belief in the divinity of Christ, is in dispute. Nevertheless, the central affirmations of the Apostles' Creed, having stood the test of time, still give us a compendium of Christian wisdom.

It is not customary to link the Apostles' Creed with Christian ethics or social action. Yet its major affirmations do form a basis for this procedure, provided they are seen in the light of the Christian message as a whole. It is the purpose of this chapter to indicate how this is the case. So, I shall take up these central affirmations one by one, pointing them in the direction of a number of problems of the contemporary world. I hope thus to indicate that Christian theology—even an ancient statement of Christian theology—can be relevant to the issues of life that confront us all.

Perhaps I should say at the outset, though it should be unnecessary, that what I shall present is not the only Christian position. I think my theology is fairly close to the central, middle-of-the-road stream of historic Christianity, but when it comes to applications there will certainly be wide differences of opinion.

I Believe in God

To begin with an affirmation which is not only time honored but accepted by most Christians: "I believe in God the Father Almighty, maker of heaven and earth." This means that the whole world, with its sorry aspects as well as its glorious ones, is God's world. All nature is God's; all people are God's people. This does not mean that God is responsible for human sin or for the mass of human misery that we ought to be laboring to eliminate. It certainly does not mean that everything is as God wills to have it in his world. I do not attempt to solve in a sentence the baffling problem of evil; but my general position is that most, if not all, of it is caused by man's misuse of God's great gifts of human freedom, social relatedness, and natural order, and that he calls us to work with him toward the perfecting of an unfinished creation.[1]

To turn to the more positive aspects of the belief that this is God's world, created in its basic structure by God the Father Almighty and hence a creation for human good, this points to a central emphasis on stewardship. This is expressly stated in the Genesis story of creation in the injunction to "fill the earth and subdue it; and have dominion" over everything on, under, or over the earth. This obviously must include the subduing of more recalcitrant elements and having dominion over more forms of value in nature than the author of this great prose poem could possibly have anticipated. Yet the principle is there, deeply embedded in biblical faith in the covenant relation of the Old Testament and presupposed in the new covenant inaugurated by Jesus. The parable of the talents is perhaps its most explicit statement in the Gospels, but man's responsibility to God through a right use of God's gifts is implicit in the total ministry and teaching of Jesus.

This note of stewardship as a God-given responsibility in a God-given world impinges on current

[1] If the reader wishes to know further what I think on this moot theme, he will find it in my book *The Providence of God* (Nashville: Abingdon Press, 1960).

thinking at many points, but three in particular. One of these is the emphasis on the laity as the church within the world, called to serve God in the day's work through a vocation, that is, in a *calling* that is far more God-centered than is usually implied in the word "vocation" as occupation or form of employment. If this true and wholesome emphasis were taken seriously by all Christians—or if that be an unattainable ideal, by *many* Christians —it could go far toward reconstructing the economic aspects of society. It would eliminate much of the callous unconcern for persons in an industrial society and put a new zest for meaningful service into most of the world's necessary occupations. It would not replace the need of technical competence or rule out all forms of competition, and I am not suggesting that it would at once bring in Utopia. Yet if this principle of the mission of the laity in stewardship of labor, talent, and possessions were to become more general, it could go a long way toward eliminating exploitation, conflict, and hostility in a changing social order.

A second aspect of stewardship as a God-given responsibility has to do with another phrase from the Genesis story of creation: "Be fruitful and multiply." This men and women have been doing, and continue to do, at what has become an alarming rate. I find nothing in the Bible which speaks directly to the need of family limitation. Yet the principle of stewardship of God's gifts within God's world applies as directly to the sexual impulse as to any other. Without restriction of the birth rate, society appears to be inevitably on a collision course. The *Discipline* of The United Methodist Church puts it succinctly in a wise word: "We believe that planned parenthood, practiced with respect for human life, fulfills rather than violates the will of God. . . . This issue must be seen in reference to the pressing population problem now before the whole world." [2]

A third implication of the importance of stewardship in a God-given world appears in attempts of the current radical theology to encourage constructive social change without God. Obedience to Jesus is enjoined without the God of Jesus. It is, of course, obvious that it is not Christians *only* who are concerned about social evils and are working for a better world. Cooperation with other persons is imperative. Yet for Christians to engage in such action without a sense of divine mandate and hope of fulfillment is both illogical and enervating. Jesus gave us the love commandments out of his own sense of the love of God for all men. However much the direction conscience takes is shaped by the environment and social conditioning, conscience itself is the gift of God and the source of the Christian's moral imperative, whether in times of rapid social change or the most

[2] *The Book of Discipline of The United Methodist Church,* 1968, ¶ 94.

stable situations. To try to divorce it from God is to leave it floating in a sea of relativity.

In Jesus Christ

"And in Jesus Christ his only Son our Lord." To continue looking at the words of the creed, the centrality of Christ as divine Lord and Savior has more than a little relation to Christian social ethics. Though we had better not tinker with the historic wording, "his only Son" is best understood if we substitute mentally the word "unique" for "only." Jesus was unique in his vision of the nature and reality of God, of the ever-present needs of sinful and suffering humanity, and of the availability of the love of God for the forgiveness of sin and the transformation of life. Many of his teachings can be found in the Old Testament and in other high religions; nowhere else is there such a constellation of teaching, living, ministry to need across all barriers, and relationship to God in one's own person. The cross and the resurrection seal for the Christian believer what was manifest in the life of our Lord, and even though this life must be seen through the eyes of the New Testament writers, without full clarity, it is enough to convince us of his saviorhood.

It is true that Jesus addressed his message primarily to individuals and dealt only indirectly with social issues, such as are implied in the great Last Judgment scene of Matthew 25. From this

141

fact and the obvious differences between his environment and ours, it is often concluded that Jesus casts no light on today's problems except in terms of the general principle of love. This has been elaborated into a situational or contextual ethic of which relativity is the primary note. All "Thou shalts" and "Thou shalt nots," we are told, are to be cast aside and every situation judged in the light of its context.

Here I believe we must move carefully, for neither legalistic prescriptions and prohibitions nor such relativity as is now commonly advocated seem to me properly derivative from the spirit and teachings of Jesus. The love commandment is indeed the covering criterion for all else. Yet within its application Jesus has much more to teach us. To summarize here what I have dealt with elsewhere at much greater length,[3] these notes emerge from the recorded words and deeds of Jesus.

1. The ethics of Jesus are centered in his relation to God or, as we might say, in his religion. Their keynote is that the moral life flows out from the worship of God in glad obedience to his will. This ethical note is implied in his central theme of the kingdom of God, though it does not exhaust the meaning of it. The kingdom connotes both moral acceptance of God's rulership and the escha-

[3] Especially in *The Sources of Western Morality* (New York: Scribner's, 1954), Chap. IX, and in *Christian Ethics* (Nashville: Abingdon Press, 1957), Chap. III.

tological fulfillment of God's purposes. The fact that we are bidden to pray for its coming on earth presupposes that we are bidden also to act in the light of its norms.

2. Jesus imparted a fresh sense of the worth of every individual in the sight of God. Not because a person is by nature or his own achievement either good or great, but because he is precious to God, every person is of supreme worth and should be so regarded by his fellowmen. The total ministry of Jesus was aimed at the redemption of persons, whether from physical illness, mental disturbance, prejudice, or sin, because he shared the love of God for every person. This principle lies at the root of the Christian moral imperative to so remake the social order that all men may express their best and live at their highest.

3. Jesus had a clear understanding both of human sin and of human possibilities. He did not talk about sin nearly as much as did Paul, according to our records, but as John's Gospel puts it, "He himself knew what was in man" (John 2:25). Yet he also knew what man could become through the love and forgiveness of God and moral dedication to the call of God. Such a two-sided realism is very essential if, amid new forms of the perennial pull of greed and fear, either better individual lives or a better society are to be fashioned.

4. Jesus grasped the importance of combining

right motives with right fruits. The Beatitudes illustrate this. In each the first clause states an attitude, the second its reward. The blessed are the humble, the compassionate, the patient, the pure in heart, the peace-loving, those who pursue with determination the way of righteousness in the face of opposition. Jesus does not promise success in the ordinary sense, but he does promise divine support and the reward of God's approval.

5. Jesus made unqualified demands. This is not to say that he was a legalist in a moralistic sense. Yet he never watered down God's righteousness to easy human performance or to hedonistic enjoyment, as much of modern life tends to do. The life of obedient love is one of blessedness and high reward, but it is also the way of the cross.

Were we to take seriously these principles and apply them, for example, to the racial tensions of our time, where would we come out? Racial discrimination and prejudice in all its forms would need to be condemned, not only from the standpoint of human justice, but from the standpoint of God's love for every person. This would call for more love, more forbearance, more understanding on both sides of the cleavage, but not at the cost of an inertia stemming from fear of precipitating trouble. It would call for fellowship in Christ among those of different races and differing opinions, a fellowship sanctified by worshiping together the one God, and would put an end forever to racial exclusiveness in Christ's church. From this center could stem a transformation in the many institutions of society where life meets life.

Such a consummation requires, of course, political action, economic readjustment, education of the underprivileged and education of the public to their needs, and much else. These procedures are not spelled out for us in the New Testament. God expects us to use our minds, our voices, and our votes. Yet beneath all such action the basic requirement is the will to equality, freedom, and justice, all of these actuated by love. Such a motive and outlook are found at their highest in the faith and the moral insights of Jesus.

In some measure, such a movement is discernible in our time. Even amid violence and the resulting backlash, racial understanding and justice inch their way forward. These are not God's methods as we see them in Jesus, but God is not absent from the struggle. With a wider and deeper acceptance of the way of Christ, such a social change could come about as would transform bitterness into joy, and bring harmony and mutuality to a strife-torn land.

I Believe in the Holy Spirit

The Holy Spirit, or Holy Ghost in traditional diction, has tended to be regarded by Christians as a somewhat "ghostly" concept—seldom denied, seldom very clearly understood. The concept has a firm place in the Christian doctrine of the Trinity, but seldom impinges on Christian social ethics.

The Holy Spirit has long been conceived as the life-giver and sanctifier, giving guidance, comfort, and strength to the individual in his need and upbuilding him in the Christian life. The Spirit is the Paraclete, the Comforter, Counselor, Advocate, Helper—it is hard to find a single word to express what Jesus promised to his followers in the Last Supper discourse. He is, furthermore, the Spirit of truth, to teach and to give guidance into all truth, bearing witness to the Son from the Father when the Son is no longer visibly present (John 14:16, 26; 15:26; 16:7-11).

These are great concepts, and I see no reason to disavow them. What they add up to is the continuing presence and nearness of the God who has come to the world in Christ and who will be with his people throughout all time. Paul's frequent identification of the Holy Spirit with the risen and living Christ makes sense, and coheres with the last words of the Gospel of Matthew: "Lo, I am with you always, to the close of the age."

This promise has brought help to countless individuals. Furthermore, the Holy Spirit is often conceived as at work within Christ's church. But can we find the Holy Spirit as our helper within the rough-and-tumble of a rapidly changing social order? Is not this the place for shrewd calculation, technical knowledge, political and economic action instead of any such intangible source of power?

My contention is that if we believe that God is at work in history—a basic tenet of Christian faith—then there is no need to deny the presence or the work of the Holy Spirit in matters of Christian social action. In times of critical decision divine guidance is certainly needed, not as a substitute for careful thought and planning but as reinforcement and direction. We need the Holy Spirit to keep us patient and persevering when things go wrong and all the odds seem stacked against us. We need the Holy Spirit to keep us humble when things go as we had hoped to have them. In short, we need to have the awareness of God's presence and God's undergirding power in every circumstance.

Granted that we are at all times in need of the Holy Spirit, we are in special need in times when the forces of change are moving with great rapidity. In more sober language we may speak of the need of guidance by goals, values, and well-grounded fresh perspectives. Translated into religious language, this means guidance by "the Spirit of truth." Much of the chaos of contemporary life comes from the disregard of such perspectives. Yet it is essentially the function of the Holy Spirit to make us feel the presence of God in every new situation and thus maintain a sane, strong, and steady vision within changing circumstances.

Some of the religious allusions often made in political addresses are obviously lugged in, put there to curry favor in a nation that in spite of a pervasive secularism still gives lip-and-ear service to the God of our fathers. But not all. When Abraham Lincoln spoke—or to cite a more recent great martyred President, John F. Kennedy—the biblical citations and references to God seemed to ring true. They were fallible men, but through them the Holy Spirit spoke. So it may be with us who are lesser figures, provided our insights are guided by the best wisdom available to us.

The Holy Catholic Church

"I believe . . . in the holy catholic church, the communion of saints, the forgiveness of sins." This trilogy of affirmations I propose to group together because of their interrelatedness. The communion of saints is an ambiguous term with various meanings, perhaps most commonly thought of as referring to a mystic fellowship of the perfect and the just in heaven. In this sense it is synonymous with the "church triumphant" in contrast with the "church militant." Yet this is not its only meaning. The term most certainly includes also, not the perfect on earth of whom there are none, but the faithful and devoted followers of Christ throughout all time and in every place. If we substitute for "the communion of saints" a more familiar and

148

hence more meaningful term, "the fellowship of the faithful," then it becomes synonymous with Christ's true church, though these "saints" may not be identical with the members of the visible institution.

If one is a Catholic with a capital C, he may believe that the church can forgive sins through the delegated authority of the priesthood to give absolution. This, however, is not my reason for linking forgiveness with "the holy catholic church." As a Protestant I believe that the church is an indispensable channel for the mediation of God's grace to sinning, suffering, stumbling humanity, but not the only channel. Persons are brought to penitence and the readiness both to give and to receive forgiveness through understanding professional counsel and through plain human friendliness which "accepts the unacceptable" and hence leads to self-acceptance and a new approach to life. Yet the church not only has long been, but still is, the primary medium for this redemptive change.

Both in personal living and in great social issues, there is no substitute for the humble recognition of one's own shortcomings and the willingness to forgive others for theirs. Without this spirit on both sides there is no reconciliation, and where there is no reconciliation there is no peace. If this reconciliation is brought about by agents of what

Paul Tillich called the "latent" rather than the "manifest" church, is it not still God's work?

This peace may be the "peace of God, which passes all understanding" of which Paul wrote from a Roman dungeon, undoubtedly referring to peace within the soul of the Christian. This is by no means to be disparaged in our restive, uneasy generation, in which hosts of individuals are "lost" in a morass of meaninglessness. Yet it is not inner peace alone that calls for that reconciliation of which the prime ingredients are penitence and forgiveness.

Note that I said reconciliation, not conciliation, appeasement, or the absence of open conflict. These situations come about too often through fear on the weaker side and the crushing power of superior force on the other. This is not to say that there is no occasion when force is needed—that is another question. The issue here is the need of reconciliation, mutual understanding and goodwill in *any* situation.

Whether the issue is tension within the home, between friends and neighbors, in labor relations, between the races, or among the nations, reconciliation is essential before there can be any real settlement of conflict. We are not required by Christian faith to approve our enemies' acts or to be blind and deaf to their occurrence. What we are enjoined to do is to love our enemies and to seek, in humble recognition of our own short-comings, to be helpful to them through any channels that may be open.

To generate such a spirit is a major task, though by no means the only task, of the churches. Much needs to be done through education, legislation, and the stewardship of possessions to translate attitudes of reconciliation into constructive social change. Yet without such a spirit, conflict degenerates into endless bickering, violence, and finally the colossal destructiveness of war. If the church can be the mediator and exemplar of attitudes of penitence, forgiveness, and reconciliation, this is no mean service within the social struggles of our time.

But to look further at "the holy catholic church," how holy is the church today? And how catholic? The frequent complaint is that it lacks both of these qualities and is so self-centered and ingrown that one may as well give up on it and throw one's energies into the social struggle beyond its doors. There are complex causes for the fact that many of the church's ablest potential leaders either leave the ministry or bypass it, but a constant barrage of such charges of irrelevance certainly affects this situation.

Whether the church is *holy* depends on the meaning attached to the term. It is not perfect either in its ecclesiastical structure or its fallible human membership. Though some communions hold that the church as the mystical body of Christ cannot sin, this is not the Protestant position. The church in its corporate relationships, however much reformed, is always in need of reformation.

Yet in a very important sense, the church is holy. It is the carrier of a gospel that is of God. We have this treasure, to be sure, in earthen vessels. Yet in spite of the many weaknesses of Christ's followers, there is something of Christ's spirit in this community that bears his name. Because of this gospel, which again and again bursts forth in new light and power, "the powers of death shall not prevail against it." Recent movements in both the Catholic and Protestant churches toward inward renewal and greater outreach in service to the world may well be regarded as the Spirit of God at work in the current scene. The liturgical renewal; the coffee house movement; the various forms of chaplaincy; the effort to eliminate urban ghettos in the North, racial power structures in the South, and poverty pockets everywhere are not without their marks of earthiness. Yet in a true sense such endeavors give evidence of a holy concern within Christ's church.

Whether the church is *catholic* is also in part a matter of semantics. Divided though the church of Christ is, it is still the church universal. It is clearly intended by God to be world embracing, in both the geographical and cultural connotations of "the world." Though it has not achieved this goal in either sense, it has made amazing advances in the first with some retrogression in the second. Because of this paradox we find ourselves in the most ecumenical and the most secular periods of the church's history at the same time.

These movements are not unrelated. Great developments in communication and transportation have brought the world, including the world's churches, into closer contact, and hitherto unsuspected common grounds have been discovered. At the same time, technology and its products have become for many persons their "ultimate concern." The resolution of the paradox has no single key, but at least one demand is clear. This is that cooperation of the churches in worship, study, fellowship, and action is basic to their service to the world.

This is being said today on many fronts. It has not been better said than in the section on "Tradition and Traditions" in the Fourth World Conference on Faith and Order. There we read: "Catholicity, as a gift of God's grace, calls us to a task. It is a concept of immense richness. . . . It can be sought and received only through consciousness of, and caring for, the wholeness of Christ's body, through witness for Christ's Lordship over every area of human life, and through compassionate identification with every man in his own particular need." [4]

And the Life Everlasting

This is both too large a question to discuss at length as this presentation comes to a close, and at the same time one which cannot be omitted. The Christian's belief in the life everlasting is as far removed as anything could be from the "pie in the sky" assumptions with which it has been identified. It is a reverent, humble, and trusting confidence that neither life nor death can separate us from the love of God and that in his good keeping all is well.

The bearing of this on a theology of social change is less directly evident than in the previous affirmations of the creed. Yet it is present. My honored professor, the late William Ernest Hocking, once remarked that a wholly this-worldly perspective "lacks the resonance of a divine concern in its inward vitality." The sentence stuck in my memory, and I believe it to be profoundly true. Although those persons who believe in the life everlasting have no monopoly on good works, it has been my observation that those who labor most persistently, and if necessary suffer most, without losing hope or courage are those who have this

[4] The Fourth World Conference on Faith and Order, Montreal, 1963. Report edited by P. C. Rodger and L. Vischer, p. 59.

resonance of a divine concern. When one's faith and vision, turned as they must be and should be toward this world and its needs, have a perspective not circumscribed by the limits of time and biological existence, then God is in the action and every effort has an open end.

Index